They Went That-A-Way

PARAMOUNT PRESENTS IN VistaVision

BURT LANCASTER · KIRK DOUGLAS

IN HAL WALLIS' PRODUCTION OF

GUNFIGHT AT THE O.K. CORRAL

CO-STARRING · RHONDA FLEMING · JO VAN FLEET · JOHN IRELAND

DIRECTED BY JOHN STURGES · SCREEN PLAY BY LEON URIS · MUSIC COMPOSED AND CONDUCTED BY DIMITRI TIOMPKINS
TECHNICOLOR® · DISTRIBUTED BY CINEMA INTERNATIONAL CORPORATION

They Went That-A-Way

Editor: Ann Lloyd

Consultant Editor: David Robinson

Orbis Publishing · London

Contents

The Golden West *Jeffrey Richards* 7

Old Timer *Olivier Eyquem* 11

The Covered Wagon *Allen Eyles* 12

Tumbleweeds *Jeffrey Richards* 14

Saloon Sirens and Prairie Roses *David Thomson* 16

Kings of the Wild Frontier *Robert Reiner* 20

Lonesome Trail *Allen Eyles* 25

How John Ford's West was Won *Bertrand Tavernier* 29

Stagecoach *David Robinson* 34

The Codes of the West *Colin McArthur* 36

A Man, a Horse and a Gun *Allen Eyles* 39

Home on the Range *Jeffrey Richards* 43

The Ox-Bow Incident *Clyde Jeavons* 46

The Great Western Myth *Tom Milne* 48

My Darling Clementine *Olivier Eyquem* 52

Mann of the West *Julian Petley* 54

High Noon in the West *Joel Finler* 57

The Gunfighter *Richard Schickel* 60

The Ranown Cycle *Richard T. Jameson* 62

High Noon *Graham Fuller* 64

Lonesome Cowboy *Richard T. Jameson* 66

The Searchers *Graham Fuller* 70

'John Wayne, American' *Graham Fuller* 72

Rio Bravo *Allen Eyles* 76

Butch Cassidy and the Sundance Kid *John Thompson* 78

The Wild Bunch *Tim Pulleine* 80

Pizza (or Pasta) Westerns *David Thomson* 83

Little Big Man *Graham Fuller* 86

Country and Westerns *Neil Sinyard* 89

Heaven's Gate *Sally Hibbin* 92

Index 94

Acknowledgments 96

Abbreviations used in text

add: additional; **adv:** advertising; **anim:** animation;
art dir: art direction; **ass:** assistant; **assoc:** associate; **chor:** choreography;
col: colour process; **comm:** commentary; **cont:** continuity; **co-ord:** co-ordination;
cost: costume; **dec:** decoration; **des:** design; **dial:** dialogue; **dial dir:** dialogue direction;
dir: direction; **doc:** documentary; **ed:** film editing; **eng:** engineer; **ep:** episode;
exec: executive; **loc:** location; **lyr:** lyrics; **man:** management; **mus:** music; **narr:** narration;
photo: photography; **prod:** production; **prod co:** production company; **prod sup:** production
supervision; **rec:** recording; **rel:** released; **r/t:** running time; **sc:** scenario/screenplay/script;
sd: sound; **sp eff:** special effects; **sup:** supervision; **sync:** synchronization;
sys: system. Standard abbreviations for countries are used. Most are
self-evident but note: A = Austria; AUS = Australia; GER = Germany
and West Germany after 1945; E.GER = East Germany.

The golden West

The silent Westerns carried on where real life left off, since the world they portrayed, although it still existed, was rapidly fading away in a glow of nostalgia

The Western is one of the finest creations of American culture, and the cowboy one of the great macho heroes of the world. Historically, the supreme era of the cowboy was short. It lasted from the end of the American Civil War in 1865 to the 1880s, when the cry was for beef to feed the hungry, growing nation. These were the days of the epic cattle drives up the famous trails like the Goodnight and the Chisholm, the days of the cattle empires, of the wide-open cow towns like Abilene and Dodge City, of range wars and murderous rivalries – the raw material of cowboy legend. But disastrous weather, bad management and the collapse of the beef market put an end to the boom; the arrival of homesteaders and the spread of barbed wire terminated the open range. Cowboys continued to exist and to ply their trade; but the old expansive, free-wheeling life had ended. Many cowboys moved on and the destination of some of them was Hollywood. By the Twenties, it was estimated that 500 a year came to Hollywood from ranches in Arizona and Colorado that were going broke.

The earliest Westerns therefore not only reconstructed the story and the life-style of the Old West – they overlapped with it and actually continued it. Real-life western characters appeared in films about their exploits: outlaws such as Al Jennings and Emmett Dalton and lawmen such as Bill Tilghman, last of the great western marshals. Tilghman made a number of films, actually interrupting the shooting of one of them to round up some bank robbers, thus mingling fantasy and reality with a vengeance. For the epic film *North of 36* (1924), the director Irvin Willat staged the first longhorn cattle drive for nearly thirty-five years, exactly replicating the conditions of the drives in the 1870s.

But for all the documentary-style realism of some of these Western reconstructions, the mass audience went to Westerns primarily for dashing heroes and plenty of action, preferably in impressive locations. So the films that the real-life cowboys helped to make in Hollywood gave worldwide currency to a romantic archetype which had been established even before the film industry came into being. The cowboy was seen as the embodiment of the virtues of the American frontier. These had been described by the historian Frederick Jackson Turner in 1893:

'That coarseness and strength combined with acuteness and inquisitiveness; that practical, inventive turn of mind, quick to find expedients; that masterful grasp of material things, lacking in the artistic but powerful to effect great ends; that restless, nervous energy; that dominant individualism working for good and for evil, and withal that buoyancy and exuberance which comes with freedom.'

These characteristics were blended with the essential elements of the chivalric gentleman of the Old World – courtesy, bravery and nobility – to create an ideal Westerner. This image was perfected by three men, all Easterners, all friends, all intoxicated by the heroic vision of the West and all destined to influence the Hollywood version of it. Owen Wister, a Philadelphian, made the cowboy the hero of his novel *The Virginian*, published in 1902. It was the first serious Western novel and gave the cowboy pride of place over the previously preferred heroes, the dime-novel favourites – the outlaw, the lawman, the pioneer, the trapper and the scout. Frederic Remington, a New Yorker, in his

Above: Prentiss Ingraham wrote the dime novels signed by Buffalo Bill as well as 200 stories about the popular Western hero. Below: in The Covered Wagon, *the wagon train unwisely makes a stand against the Indians in a box canyon, open to attack from above*

paintings of cattle drives and round-ups, gunfights and hold-ups, recorded a West made up of swirls of action and colour, with manly cowboys at its centre. Theodore Roosevelt, aristocratic President, explorer and big-game hunter, preached in his life and in his books a militant Anglo-Saxonism of which the cowboy was the proud exemplar. The first epic Western film, *The Covered Wagon* (1923), was to be dedicated to his memory. The impact of the cowboy can be gauged from the fact that the terms 'Western film' and 'cowboy film' became interchangeable, although many Western films actually featured no cowboys as such.

Although the cowboy was being ennobled for the first time, the process was built on the tradition of the dime novels. From the 1860s onwards, as the West seized the imagination of America, a flood of cheap novels, written according to a few formulas, had poured from the presses, dramatizing and romanticizing the adventures of real and fictional Western heroes. Dime novels became one of the primary sources of film content, reinforced by stage melodramas with Western settings and the Wild West shows which popularized what became the great set-pieces of Western films – the stagecoach chase, the wagon-train attack and the cavalry charge.

One figure tapped all these sources of inspiration – Colonel William F. Cody, 'Buffalo Bill' himself. A real-life scout and buffalo hunter, he was taken up by the leading dime novelist, Ned Buntline, who started a long series of novels describing his fictional adventures. Cody took to the stage in 1872 in a rather bad melodrama called *The Scouts of the Plains* and, discovering that he lacked aptitude as an actor, launched his celebrated Wild West show in 1883. Towards the end of his life, he brought the wheel full circle by producing and starring in a film of his Western exploits, made in 1913 and known by various titles, including *The Adventures of Buffalo Bill*. His career is the perfect demonstration of how historical reality shaded into cinematic fiction.

It was inevitable that films would follow the lead of the stage and the printed page, and Westerns became a staple of the new entertainment medium

Above: Frederic Remington's 1899 painting Missing *depicts a cavalry trooper captured by hostile Indians and unlikely to survive for long, since Indians soon killed their prisoners. Top right: an encounter between Indian warriors in* The Way of a Mother *(1913), supervised by Thomas H. Ince. Right: G. M. Anderson as Broncho Billy (right) in a 1913 story of a tenderfoot who gets tired of being pushed around and becomes a crack shot. Far right: in* White Oak *(1921), William S. Hart plays Oak Miller, a gambler obsessed with visiting revenge on the man who deceived his sister; the villain is finally killed by an Indian chief whose daughter he has betrayed. Below right: Harry Carey as a good-hearted outlaw in Ford's* The Scarlet Drop *(1918)*

early on. The first recorded Western is a one-minute vignette entitled *Cripple Creek Bar Room*, produced in 1898. The first Western story film, *The Great Train Robbery*, followed in 1903. Directed by Edwin S. Porter, it was actually filmed in New Jersey but told a classic story of robbery, chase and retribution. It had enormous success at the box-office and was extensively imitated. One thing it did not have was a hero. But in the cast was an actor called Gilbert M. Anderson, who was soon ready to remedy this defect. Overcoming an initial tendency to fall off his horse, he saw the potential in the cowboy hero, launched a new company (Essanay) and took a film unit off first to Colorado and then to California, where he began producing one- and two-reel Westerns, many of them featuring Anderson himself as a sentimental tough guy called Broncho Billy. Anderson, who appeared in hundreds of Broncho Billy films between 1908 and 1916, thus became the first Western hero. Business problems kept him off the screen for over a year and when he

of his romanticism, plots that were sentimental, melodramatic and heavily moralistic. In his films he played a succession of ramrod-straight, grim-visaged badmen with names like Black Deering, Blaze Tracey and Draw Egan, who were underneath it all chivalric and sentimental and whose moral regeneration was a central theme of the stories. In *Hell's Hinges* (1916), he actually burns down a sinful town, in a sequence eerily prefiguring Clint Eastwood's *High Plains Drifter* (1973). Hart's horse Fritz became the first of a long line of star movie horses who became as well-known as their riders. But Hart's popularity waned and the piety, sentimentality and comparatively slow pace of his films came to seem increasingly old-fashioned with the rise of a very different sort of star – Tom Mix. Hart refused to change his style and after a final film, *Tumbleweeds* (1925), he retired. *Tumbleweeds* represents the triumphant summation of Hart's vision of the West and takes place symbolically against the background of the end of the open range and the arrival of the homesteaders. It also contains a stunningly executed and majestically shot set-piece, the Cherokee Strip land rush, which ranks with the best of its kind in the genre.

Where Hart had prided himself on the authenticity of his films, Tom Mix's films were pure fantasy. He has first entered films in mid-1909 as a stockman and supporting player in a rodeo picture, *Ranch Life in the Great Southwest* (1910), and from then until 1917 he worked for the Selig

Westerns drew for inspiration on dime novels, stage melodramas, rodeos and Wild West shows

company, turning out something like a hundred Westerns, one- and two-reelers, which he often wrote and directed as well as starring in. But in 1917 he moved to Fox and his career took off. The inspiration of his films was the circus and the Wild West show, where Hart's had been Victorian melodrama and photographic realism. Tom Mix's cowboy hero, flamboyantly costumed, involved himself in fast-moving, far-fetched stories, strong on stunts, action and comedy. Fleet of foot, keen of eye and effortlessly gallant, Tom Mix became the Doug Fairbanks of the sagebrush. He set the style and pattern for the Westerns of a host of rivals and imitators. Indeed from his own supporting casts emerged Buck Jones and George O'Brien, who were both to be promoted as Western stars by Fox.

Westerns received a tremendous boost in 1923 when Paramount released the first indisputable Western epic, *The Covered Wagon*. Based on Emerson Hough's novel, it began as a conventional programmer about a wagon boss falsely accused of a crime by his rival for the heroine's affections, but expanded to become the saga of wagons westward on the Oregon Trail in 1848. It exists now only in an incomplete print. Nevertheless it can be said that despite such assets as the grandeur of Karl Brown's photography, the documentary look imparted by eight weeks' location shooting to such large-scale action sequences as the wagon train's departure, the river crossing and a buffalo hunt, and the rich character comedy of Ernest Torrence and Tully Marshall as two old frontiersmen, it is a flawed film. The director James Cruze, whatever his strengths, was weak on action highlights and suspense, and the Indian attack on the wagon train and its rescue are clumsily mishandled.

But the film was a great box-office success, and it emboldened Fox to turn its new Western *The Iron*

returned he found that new idols had risen and his career faded.

The artistic possibilities in the Western became clear in the work of two of the cinema's great innovators – D. W. Griffith and Thomas H. Ince. Griffith in his years at Biograph brought his increasingly sophisticated technique and powerful visual sense to Westerns, imbuing such projects as *The Last Drop of Water* (1911), *The Massacre* (1913) and *The Battle at Elderbush Gulch* (1914) with truly epic qualities. Thomas H. Ince, the first producer to insist on fully detailed and comprehensive scripts for the guidance of the production team as well as the actors, and an organizational genius when it came to staging large-scale action, hired the Miller Brothers 101 Ranch Real Wild West Show, to provide him with a ready-made stock company of cowboys and Indians, longhorn cattle, stage-coaches and wagons. He turned out Westerns from his Inceville studios, one of the most successful of which was *Custer's Last Raid* (1912), directed by and starring Francis Ford (though Ince officially took the directorial credit). This film so impressed Carl Laemmle that he lured Ford away from Ince and set him to work at Universal, which was to become one of the major producers of Westerns. But Francis Ford was eventually to be eclipsed as a director by his younger brother John Ford and as an actor by Harry Carey and then Hoot Gibson, who both starred in many popular Westerns for Universal, some of them directed by the up-and-coming John (then known as Jack) Ford.

Ince, however, found a more-than-adequate replacement for Francis Ford in William S. Hart, who entered films in 1914 at the age of 44. Previously a stage actor, who had appeared not only in Shakespeare and *Ben-Hur* but also in such popular Western stage melodramas as *The Squaw Man* and *The Virginian*, Hart was an incurable romantic. He had been raised in the West, loved it and wanted to depict it realistically on the screen. First with Ince and later with Paramount, he succeeded in his aim, giving his films a gritty surface realism of austere, dusty townships and authentic cowboy costume and accoutrements. But with this went another side

Above: a dime-novel-reading cowboy (Ken Maynard) acts as guide to a circus in The Wagon Show *(1928) and becomes its star rider. Below: after an Indian attack, the train returns to the railhead in John Ford's* The Iron Horse. *Bottom: production shot of* The Vanishing American, *sympathetic to the Navajo Indians and filmed in authentic locations*

Horse (1924) into an epic. So the familiar story of a young man seeking the murderer of his father burgeoned into a full-scale reconstruction of the building of the transcontinental railroad. In John Ford, Fox had a director who could combine visual sweep and exciting action sequences, rich comedy interludes and acutely-observed details of everyday life to counterpoint the epic theme. In George O'Brien, Ford found a wholly convincing Western star, virile, natural and likeable. The result was one of the great achievements of the silent cinema. Other epics followed, such as Irvin Willat's *North of 36* and James Cruze's *The Pony Express* (1925). But none of them achieved the success of *The Covered Wagon* and *The Iron Horse*, and it became clear that large-scale evocations of nationalistic sentiment were not entirely to the public's taste. Interestingly, after his magisterial land-rush epic *Three Bad Men* (1926), John Ford was not to make another Western until *Stagecoach* (1939).

Programme Westerns, however, flourished and production of them trebled in the year following *The Covered Wagon*. Films on the streamlined, action-packed Tom Mix model were what was required, and in his wake a posse of immortals galloped across the screen. These were the men in white hats riding white horses, the paladins of the prairies, the idols of the Saturday matinées.

MGM launched a group of historical Westerns starring the stalwart Colonel Tim McCoy, a former Indian agent who had handled the Indians used in the making of *The Covered Wagon*. At First National, Ken Maynard starred in rousing Western adventures, whose spectacular set-piece highlights were to be reused constantly as stock footage throughout the Thirties. At FBO, Fred Thomson, a former Presbyterian minister and Boy Scout leader, now forgotten but idolized in his day, rode and fought his way into the hearts of a legion of young admirers. From Paramount between 1921 and 1928 (and thereafter in the sound era) came an impressive series of adaptations of the novels of Zane Grey, arguably the most popular of Western writers. With classic plots and evocative titles like *The Thundering Herd*, *The Vanishing American* and *Wild Horse Mesa* (all 1925), they generally starred steely-eyed Jack Holt or rugged Richard Dix. They also benefited from being filmed, as the contract with Grey specifically demanded, on the actual locations of the stories.

By 1926, however, a glut of cheap Westerns took the edge off the public demand and the coming of sound apparently signalled their doom. Short on that essential commodity, dialogue, they were dubbed old-fashioned and over-romantic. The vogue was for bang-up-to-date films that could exploit the new medium, and Westerns were eclipsed by gangster films with their screeching cars and machine-gun battles and by musicals – 'all-talking, all-singing, all-dancing'. Production of Westerns was cut by as much as 75 per cent and in 1929 *Photoplay* magazine declared: 'Western novel and motion picture heroes have slunk away into the brush, never to return.'
JEFFREY RICHARDS

Old-timer

Walter Brennan was one of Hollywood's most popular and energetic actors and was capable of playing many varied roles. During his long career he won no less than three Academy Awards as Best Supporting Actor – *Come and Get It* (1936), *Kentucky* (1938) and *The Westerner* (1940).

He was born in 1894 and began working as an extra in the mid-Twenties at the same time as his friend Gary Cooper. In 1927 he began to make a name for himself in B Westerns. This kind of film suited him and he continued to play in them although he did not make them his particular speciality. Prior to World War I, Brennan had done his apprenticeship in vaudeville and gained confidence and exuberance as a result of his acting as well as acquiring a hard punch. These rumbustious qualities found a natural outlet in the rustic and colourful characters which Westerns were to offer him from *Northwest Passage* (1940) to *Support Your Local Sheriff* (1969). In *Rio Bravo* (1959), for instance, he played the part of Stumpy, a cantankerous, helpless old deputy. It was a part which was to be one of the most celebrated of his career.

Brennan's first main role was in 1935 in *The Wedding Night*, and he was put under contract by Samuel Goldwyn as the perfect contrast to actors such as John Wayne, Spencer Tracy, Gary Cooper and Joel McCrea. The sobriety of these great stars emphasized the open-heartedness of his acting; the famous 'clucking' in *Rio Bravo*, the superbly theatrical homilies in *Sergeant York* (1941), the uncontrollable chattering in *To Have and Have Not* (1944) and his philosophical speeches in *Red River* (1948) stood out when contrasted with the tight-lipped monolithic performances of the stars. Often Brennan acted as a kind of Greek Chorus. He was happy to play the part of the busybody giving endless unsolicited advice and continually interrupting others to state opinions to which nobody payed the slightest attention. There was something comical about him; his apparent naivety made it hard for people to take him completely seriously. Nevertheless, his humanity always rose to the surface and his rural origins assured him a consistent genuineness.

Brennan willingly put his films into two categories; those in which he wore false teeth and those in which he did not. Having been wounded and gassed during World War I, he suffered afterwards from delicate health – which, perhaps, encouraged him to make the roles of grumbling old men his particular forte, although he could act a great variety of parts if he wanted to.

On many occasions he showed the extent of his talent, undertaking with perfect seriousness completely different parts. In *My Darling Clementine* (1946) his stiff, cutting performance and his menacing appearance were a stark contrast to his customary good nature. Nor should one forget his magnificently dignified and totally credible performance in Fritz Lang's *Hangmen Also Die!* (1943), in which he played the part of an intellectual humanist. As a whole his career must be acknowledged as one of the richest ever followed in Hollywood.

After *Rio Bravo*, Brennan spaced out his appearances. He retired from the cinema after making a last Western, *Support Your Local Sheriff*, although he continued to work regularly on television. He died in 1974 having made more than 120 films.

OLIVIER EYQUEM

Top left: Walter Brennan as the garrulous old sea-captain in To Have and Have Not. *Above: in* The Far Country *(1954), Brennan is the long-standing sidekick of Wyoming rancher, James Stewart*

Filmography
1927 Tearin' into Trouble; The Ridin' Rowdy. **'28** The Ballyhoo Buster; Smilin' Guns. **'29** The Lariat Kid; One Hysterical Night; The Long Long Trail; The Shannons of Broadway. **'30** The King of Jazz. **'31** Dancing Dynamite; Neck and Neck. **'32** Law and Order; Texas Cyclone; Two-Fisted Law; The All American (GB: Spirit of a Nation). **'33** Man of Action; Silent Men; Kiss Before the Mirror; Fighting for Justice; Sing, Sinner, Sing; One Year Later; The Invisible Man. **'34** Good Dame (GB: Good Girl); Half a Sinner. **'35** Northern Frontier; Law Beyond the Range; The Wedding Night; Bride of Frankenstein; Lady Tubbs (GB: The Gay Lady); Man on the Flying Trapeze (GB: The Memory Expert); Barbary Coast; Seven Keys to Baldpate. **'36** Three Godfathers; These Three; The Moon's Our Home; Fury; The Prescott Kid; Come and Get It (reissued as Roaring Timber); Banjo on My Knee. **'37** She's Dangerous; When Love is Young; The Affairs of Cappy Ricks; Wild and Woolly. **'38** The Buccaneer; The Adventures of Tom Sawyer; The Texans; Mother Carey's Chickens; The Cowboy and the Lady; Kentucky. **'39** The Story of Vernon and Irene Castle; They Shall Have Music (GB: Melody of Youth); Stanley and Livingstone; Joe and Ethel Turp Call on the President. **'40** Northwest Passage; Maryland; The Westerner; Nice Girl? **'41** Meet John Doe; Sergeant York; Swamp Water (GB: The Man Who Came Back); Rise and Shine. **'42** The Pride of the Yankees; Stand By for Action (GB: Cargo of Innocents). **'43** Slightly Dangerous; Hangmen Also Die!; The Last Will and Testament of Tom Smith (short); The North Star (reissued as Armoured Attack). **'44** Home in Indiana; To Have and Have Not; The Princess and the Pirate. **'45** Dakota. **'46** A Stolen Life; Centennial Summer; Nobody Lives Forever; My Darling Clementine. **'47** Driftwood. **'48** Scudda-Hoo! Scudda-Hay! (G.B. Summer Lightning); Red River; Blood on the Moon. **'49** The Green Promise (GB: Raging Waters); Brimstone; Task Force. **'50** Singing Guns; Ticket to Tomahawk; Curtain Call at Cactus Creek (GB: Take the Stage); The Showdown; Surrender. **'51** Best of the Badmen; Along the Great Divide; The Wild Blue Yonder (GB: Thunder Across the Pacific). **'52** Return of the Texan; Lure of the Wilderness. **'53** Sea of Lost Ships. **'54** Drums Across the River; Four Guns Across the Border; The Far Country. **'55** Bad Day at Black Rock; Come Next Spring; At Gunpoint (GB: Gunpoint!). **'56** Glory; Goodbye My Lady; The Proud Ones. **'57** The Way to the Gold; Tammy and the Bachelor (GB: Tammy); God is My Partner. **'59** Rio Bravo. **'62** How the West Was Won. **'65** Those Calloways. **'66** The Oscar. **'67** The Gnome-Mobile; Who's Minding the Mint? **'68** The One and Only Genuine Original Family Band. **'69** Support Your Local Sheriff.

Although the great migration westward across North America in the mid-nineteenth century had been treated in earlier Westerns such as *Wagon Tracks* (1919), which starred William S. Hart, *The Covered Wagon* was the first film to reconstruct the experience on the scale of the historical events and to emphasize the epic nature of the achievement.

It was filmed almost entirely on location, mostly on the borders of Utah and Nevada, under conditions that were at times as arduous as those suffered by the original pioneers. This was a striking departure from the standard procedure of closely supervised studio shooting, to which only Robert Flaherty's *Nanook of the North* (1922) offered a real precedent. Natural occurrences such as an unexpected snowfall were worked into the script. A river crossing was staged exactly as the original travellers achieved it by caulking the wagons and driving them across. Real Indians, 750 of them, were recruited as well as 1000 local inhabitants, and most of the 500 wagons used were genuine and not built for the film. Considerable historical research was undertaken to make the film look as convincingly authentic as possible.

The project was made possible by the enthusiasm of Jesse L. Lasky, himself the grandson of a pioneer. As vice-president in charge of production at Famous Players-Lasky, he won the support of the president, Adolph Zukor, to provide a budget five times that of a normal Western at a period when public interest in the genre was on the wane. Thereafter, it was the drive and passion of the director James Cruze that bulldozed the film through to completion, although Lasky then intervened to demand further shooting to make a stronger ending. *The Covered Wagon* finally cost a phenomenal $782,000 instead of the $500,000 originally authorized; but it was a smash hit, recouping nearly five times its cost, and as late as 1935 was generally reckoned one of the five top-grossing films to that time.

Its success revitalized the Western and encouraged Fox to shoot their railroad-building epic, *The Iron Horse* (1924), as well as to make their own wagon-train spectacular, *The Big Trail* (1930). Certainly John Ford and Raoul Walsh, as directors of these two films, showed far more imagination and artistic power than James Cruze; but it was Cruze who had shown what could be done.

The Covered Wagon no longer exists in its original form. Dramatic incidents such as a prairie fire have been removed and much documentary-like detail trimmed to give more prominence to the characters and plot. Although characterization is fairly rudimentary, the heroine shows unusual spirit and, if the hero, Banion, is too stoical in not countering the accusations of the villain, Woodhull, there is a certain vigour to their enmity with Banion barely resisting the

Directed by James Cruze, 1923
Prod co: Famous Players-Lasky. **prod:** James Cruze. **sc:** Jack Cunningham, from the novel by Emerson Hough. **photo:** Karl Brown. **ed:** Dorothy Arzner. **mus arr:** Hugo Riesenfeld. **tech adv:** Col. T. J. McCoy. **length:** 9407 ft (approx. 125 minutes). New York premiere, 16 March 1923.
Cast: Lois Wilson (*Molly Wingate*), J. Warren Kerrigan (*Will Banion*), Alan Hale (*Sam Woodhull*), Charles Ogle (*Jesse Wingate*), Ethel Wales (*Mrs Wingate*), Ernest Torrence (*Bill Jackson*), Tully Marshall (*Jim Bridger*), Guy Oliver (*Joe Dunstan*), John Fox (*Jed Wingate*).

opportunity to gouge out Woodhull's eyes after beating him in a fight, and constantly being urged by his old scout friend Bill Jackson to kill Woodhull.

River crossings and Indian attacks on encampments have become familiar ingredients of the Western, and the big scenes of *The Covered Wagon* have been criticized for their static and unadventurous use of the camera. The newsreel-like limited coverage can be seen as working in the film's favour. As Kevin Brownlow has put it:

'The fact that the camera is not ubiquitous . . . helps the initial impression that *The Covered Wagon* is a documentary record of an original trek in 1848.'

When the film is seen today, the lack of a spoken soundtrack strengthens this impression. In any case, *The Covered Wagon* makes up for a lack of camera movement by the memorable images captured by the cinematographer Karl Brown, such as the wagons of the gold seekers passing their abandoned ploughs or the shot of an Indian at night on top of a bluff, silhouetted by the white smoke of the migrants' camp fires as he shoots an arrow, or the mass of Indians charging forward in a

straight line viewed from one end.

The titles convey the flavour of the colloquial speech of the West and also point up the epic character of what is being shown. The opening title reads:

'The blood of America is the blood of pioneers – the blood of lion-hearted men and women who carved a splendid civilization out of an uncharted wilderness.'

The film also presents the Indian point of view, clearly indicating that they were fighting to preserve their way of life. Perhaps most criticism of the film as a depiction of history has centred on the wagon train's occupying a box canyon and thereby inviting Indian attack from the surrounding heights. Cruze later suggested that it showed a blunder on the leader's part but no criticism of him is made within the film.

Surprisingly, *The Covered Wagon* was never remade, although Ernest Torrence and Tully Marshall played the characters of Bill Jackson and Jim Bridger again in Paramount's *Fighting Caravans* (1931) and the studio would have made it into one of their early Vista-Vision spectaculars in 1955 if the proposed star, Alan Ladd, had not suddenly departed from the studio.

ALLEN EYLES **8**

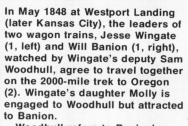

In May 1848 at Westport Landing (later Kansas City), the leaders of two wagon trains, Jesse Wingate (1, left) and Will Banion (1, right), watched by Wingate's deputy Sam Woodhull, agree to travel together on the 2000-mile trek to Oregon (2). Wingate's daughter Molly is engaged to Woodhull but attracted to Banion.

Woodhull refers to Banion's clouded past as an army officer and the two men argue (3). At the Platte river they brawl over the best way of crossing (4). Woodhull provokes the Indians by taking their ferry and shooting the owners; they destroy most of his section of the wagon train. Banion drives the other wagons across at a shallower point of the river (5).

The party crosses the Rockies to Fort Bridger, where Jim Bridger, a trader, has just learned of the discovery of gold in California. Consequently the train splits: Wingate's followers decide to continue to Oregon, while Banion leads a breakaway party heading for California. Molly is about to marry Woodhull when Bridger tells her that Banion's army reputation has been restored (6). Indians suddenly attack, wounding Molly (7) as they surround the wagon train (8). Banion's party returns to save the settlers.

By the following year Banion has struck it rich in California (9). His friend Bill Jackson foils Woodhull's final attempt to dispose of his rival. Banion rides to Oregon and is reunited with Molly (10).

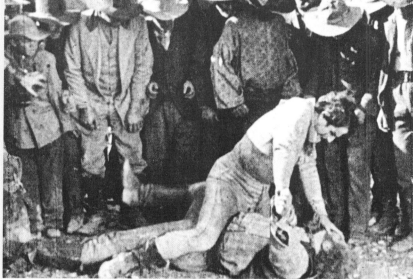

13

ASTOR PICTURES CORP
presents

The GREATEST of all WESTERN STARS

William S. HART

"TUMBLEWEEDS" His Greatest Epic

With characteristically stubborn integrity, director-actor William S. Hart refused Paramount's pleas to streamline and modernize his Westerns in the increasingly popular style of Tom Mix. Instead, he sought to vindicate his approach by setting up an independent production company, releasing through United Artists. He purchased a *Saturday Evening Post* story by Hal G. Evarts and hired C. Gardner Sullivan, who had scripted many of his early Westerns, to adapt it; to direct he called on King Baggot, the former screen idol turned director, but it is said that Hart also shared the direction without receiving any credit.

The resulting film represents the triumphant summation of Hart's art. *Tumbleweeds* combines a documentary authenticity in its sets, locales and ranch life with a plot that has all the naivety, simplicity and charm of a Victorian melodrama. Don Carver (Hart) – upright, brave, courteous, shy and resolutely unsmiling – is the epitome of the noble Western hero, saving (as he does) two orphan wolf cubs from perishing in the wild; a boy and his dog from a bullying; an old couple from dispossession; and a widow and her family from a wagon disaster during the land rush. He has the obligatory comic sidekick Kentucky Rose (Lucien Littlefield), who instigates some robust knockabout, and his courtship of the virginal Molly Lassiter (Barbara Bedford) is in the time-honoured, tongue-tied 'Aw, shucks, ma'am' tradition. Don is seen falling over the furniture, nervously smartening himself up

and sitting stiff-backed beside Molly while embarrassedly clutching a bunch of prairie flowers. She, equally sentimentally, slips a lock of his hair into her handkerchief.

The high point of the film is the staging of the Cherokee Strip land rush, arguably the finest land-rush sequence in cinema. According to the magazine *Photoplay*, it was filmed at the La Agoura Rancho, 40 miles from Hollywood, and involved some three hundred wagons and a thousand horses and men. The scene is staged, photographed and edited with such verve and creative vigour that it still takes the breath away. Close-ups of the cavalry major's watch are intercut with shots of the tense and restless settlers; as the hands of the watch approach noon a soldier stands by the cannon. When the watch reaches the appointed hour the commander lowers his arm, the cannon fires and a sea of wagons, buggies, horsemen – and even a penny-farthing cyclist – launches itself across the screen. The rhythmic intercutting of action long-shots (the thundering wagons) and close-ups of detailed incidents inexorably builds up the tension and excitement. It is then that Carver escapes from the stockade and rides hell-for-leather to catch up with the wagons on his faithful horse Fritz. At one point he even appears to be suspended in the sky as he leaps ahead of the furore.

Although the film received good reviews on its New York release, United Artists were not happy with the finished product and demanded that two reels be cut. Hart refused and so United Artists deliberately 'sabotaged' the release, only playing the film in minor cinemas. As a result Hart sued them and although he was ultimately vindicated the case was not finally

settled until 1950, four years after his death. Disheartened by the whole business, he retired to his ranch to write his memoirs.

Symbolically, perhaps, *Tumbleweeds* takes place against a background of the closing of the open range and the ending of the free and easy life of the cowboy. At one point Carver doffs his hat and declares 'Boys, it's the last of the West'. It was the last of Hart's West, but there still remained a final bow. In 1939 the film was reissued, with sound effects and musical soundtrack, and Hart spoke for the first and last time on the screen in an eight-minute prologue from his Newhall ranch. In a voice charged with all the emotion and resonance of a veteran of vintage stage melodramas, he said:

'My friends, I love the art of making motion pictures. It is as the breath of life to me. But through those hazardous feats of horsemanship that I loved so well to do for you, I received many major injuries. That, coupled with the added years of life, preclude my again doing those things that I so gloried in doing. The rush of the wind that cuts your face . . . the pounding hooves of the pursuing posse. Out there in front, a fallen tree trunk that spans a yawning chasm, with a noble animal under you that takes it in the same low, ground-eating gallop. The harmless shots of the baffled ones that remain behind, and then, the clouds of dust through which comes the faint voice of the director – ''Okay, Bill; okay. Glad you made it. Great stuff, Bill, great stuff. And say, Bill, give old Fritz a pat on the nose for me, will you?'' Oh, the thrill of it all!'

It is a moving and memorable farewell from one of the cinema's great Westerners.

JEFFREY RICHARDS

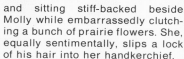

Directed by King Baggot, 1925
Prod co: William S. Hart Tumbleweed Co. **sc:** C. Gardner Sullivan, from a story by Hal G. Evarts. **photo:** Joseph August. **r/t:** 88 minutes.
Cast: William S. Hart (*Don Carver*), Barbara Bedford (*Molly Lassiter*), Lucien Littlefield (*Kentucky Rose*), J. Gordon Russell (*Noll Lassiter*), Richard R. Neill (*Freel*), Jack Murphy (*Bart Lassiter*), Lillian Leighton (*Mrs Riley*), Capt. T. E. Duncan (*Major*), Gertrude Claire (*old woman*), George Marion (*old man*), Fred Gamble (*hotel proprietor*), Turner Savage (*Riley boy*), Monte Collins (*Hicks*).

Homesteaders arrive in Caldwell, Kansas, to await the opening up of the Cherokee Strip for white settlers. Don Carver, foreman of the Box K. Ranch, supervises the round-up of the last cattle remaining on the strip and rides with his friend Kentucky into town (1). There Don saves young Bart Lassiter from being bullied (2), an act that leads to an introduction to Bart's sister Molly. Don falls in love and shyly begins to court her (3).

Molly's crooked elder brother Noll and his partner Bill Freel are 'sooners': they plan to obtain the best plot of land on the strip by illegally staking a claim prior to the land rush. When Don is sent back to search the strip for stray cattle, Freel and Noll accuse him of being a 'sooner'. A mob try to

lynch Don and he is locked up in the stockade. Next morning Noll and Freel secretly enter the strip to stake their claim.

The settlers gather for the official opening and as the land rush begins (4, 5) Don breaks out of the stockade to join it. He drives Noll and Freel off their plot and stakes it for Molly. However, she, believing that he has staked it for himself, rejects him. Sadly he tells the true story to Kentucky – who has staked his own claim and proposed to the Widow Riley (6) – and heads back to town. *En route* he comes across Noll and Freel trying to jump the claim of an elderly couple. He arrests them and turns them over to the army (7). Kentucky tells Molly the truth and she and Don are joyously reunited (8).

15

The greatest attraction of the Wild West has always been that man's wildness could be indulged without the restraints of female company. The traditional cowboy hoot and holler may be prompted by his happy partnership with a horse or the bracing quality of the fresh air, but it may also be that he's getting away from mother, wife or girlfriend. In countless Westerns the woman is left behind, and the genre can be seen as a fairly exact replica of children at play, with the mother staying out of sight preparing the milk and cookies that a hero will deserve.

In the silent Western the woman is generally kept out of the action; she becomes a figure of honour – the wistful, slender shape watching the man ride away, the uncomplaining domestic skivvy, and the object of sentimental yarns. These heroines are as lovely and helpless as the trees, as obedient as the cattle. No matter how great the reverence bestowed on them, it is difficult to believe that the men who made and liked such films did not want this state to go on for ever. When women talked, it was like getting the vote.

There are exceptions. In D. W. Griffith's *The Lonedale Operator* (1911), Blanche Sweet brings enormous zest and inventiveness to the conventional role of the threatened woman. And to the extent that *The Birth of a Nation* (1915) partakes of the Western genre, so Griffith registers the importance of women as upholders of social and racial order. Victor Sjöström's *The Wind* (1928) is a prairie film in which the harshness of life is felt as it beats upon the romantic soul of the female lead, Lillian Gish. Moreover, *The Wind* is the story of a woman's passionate experience, far more touching than most other Westerns.

As a rule, energy equalled emotion in the early Westerns, so there was no need for a woman's attitudes to intervene. It is said that at the end of James Cruze's *The Covered Wagon* (1923) mogul Jesse Lasky ordered a scene of the mother (Ethel Wales) holding the new earth in her hands to provide an emotional climax. Many movie cowboys kept a resident actress for obligatory kissing scenes: Tom Mix married his leading lady, Victoria Forde, thus ensuring her availability. The moral conflict in William S. Hart went a little further, for as the outlaw attempting to find rehabilitation Hart often faced two kinds of women – the vamp and the home-maker. Louise Glaum played his seductress and she sometimes bred a lustiness in Hart that might be visited on virgins, thus allowing him to feel guilty.

In theory the West was being civilized and made ready for pure but fertile women. But first the men made sure that they enjoyed themselves with the bar-room floozies who inhabited the saloons. The director John Ford could never decide whether he preferred rectitude or bad reputation in women. There is a smothering reverence for women in his cavalry films: in movies like *She Wore a Yellow Ribbon* (1949) the woman becomes a flag or mascot, the last sentiment surrendered or considered, a song for soldiers to sing. There are two women aboard the *Stagecoach* (1939): a whore (Claire Trevor) who has been run out of town by mean-faced hypocrites and is only fit for an outlaw like the Ringo Kid; and the officer's lady (Louise Platt), a pregnant prude, who commands the unquestioning respect of everyone, even to the extent that there is a silent pact to overlook her dullness. In *My*

SALOON SIRENS

Women in Westerns have always had a raw deal – when the men indulged themselves in wild living, they liked bad girls who showed their legs in saloons and who had a room upstairs. Conversely, there have never been more docile girlfriends than those pretty, mindless tomboys of the Western. It is only rarely that the lady out West has been able to assert her strength, character and individuality

PRAIRIE ROSES

Below: Louise Platt as the soldier's wife in Stagecoach, *with Donald Meek and John Carradine. Below left: Lillian Gish as a girl from Virginia who learns about the harsh life in a Texas prairie in* The Wind. *Above left: Chihuahua (Linda Darnell) shows the fighting spirit in* My Darling Clementine

Above: the Western was often a graveyard for actresses of talent and ambition when they risked billings like 'Roy Rogers and Trigger, with Dale Evans'. Trigger is absent though in this shot from The Golden Stallion *(1949). Below: gun-toting cowgirl – Jean Arthur as Calamity Jane in* The Plainsman

Darling Clementine (1946), the vivacious saloon-girl Chihuahua, played by Linda Darnell, is really a taboo figure. Her work and the suggestions of Mexican blood require that she stops a bullet, so Wyatt Earp (Henry Fonda) directs himself dutifully at the crisp wholesomeness of Clementine (Cathy Downs), a fit wife and mother but an empty human being.

In folklore, Earp and Doc Holliday embody the sort of civic uprightness and frontier individualism that was supposed to make the West safe for insurance companies and virgins. And their women are part of the shadow they cast: in *Gunfight at the OK Corral* (1957), Holliday has a raddled, treacherous whore (Jo Van Fleet), and Wyatt has an upstanding full-bodied red-head (Rhonda Fleming). The reality shows how incorrectly the movies portrayed the lives of frontier women. In truth Earp had three wives, the third of whom, Josephine Marcus – an energetic, good-looking, vital woman – he took from one of his political opponents in Tombstone. Thus, sexual rivalry was mixed in with the raw power-plays that culminated at the OK Corral – none of which has ever been treated in a Western.

Similarly, in films the James Brothers had mothers made of hymn books and fresh bread, and wives lost in thoughtless loyalty – all of which was in contrast to the truth. Barbara Stanwyck went against the grain of the downtrodden Western lady by playing *Annie Oakley* (1935) as a gutsy tomboy – very close to the spirit of Jean Arthur's portrayal of Calamity Jane in *The Plainsman* (1936). Annie Oakley and Jane are both lost now in the rosy glow of musicals and the personae of Mary Martin, Betty Hutton and Doris Day. But in Robert Altman's *Buffalo Bill and the Indians . . . or Sitting Bull's History Lesson* (1976) there was a whiff of reality in Geraldine Chaplin's dry and uningratiating portrait of a woman sympathetic to the Indians.

Women in Westerns rarely take action with assurance. In *Yellow Sky* (1948), when outlaws stumble upon a ghost town inhabited by a prospector and his daughter, played by Anne Baxter, she holds a rifle on one of them (Gregory Peck), but he disarms her with a simple trick that the audience sees coming. Grace Kelly's portrayal of the Quaker wife in *High Noon* (1952) shows her as so horrified by violence that she is ready to leave her new husband, the marshal (Gary Cooper). But in the end she relents, and it is her uncertain aim that dispatches the last of the gang.

Greater familiarity with guns in women is usually parody or mere gimmickry. In *Hannie Caulder* (1971), Raquel Welch plays a woman who is raped and widowed in the first sequence, and then learns gun skills, hunts down the rapists (Ernest Borgnine, Jack Elam and Strother Martin) and blasts them. This reversal of normal plot order is mere opportunism, particularly the 15 minutes during which the curvaceous star has to trudge the desert dressed in nothing more than a poncho.

It is usually the other way around: a wife is raped, killed or sometimes abducted, and the husband sets out to avenge or recover her. Woman here is the prize, the symbol of mythic ownership and also the pretext for massive guilt-free blood-letting. Budd Boetticher's Westerns starring Randolph Scott often took such a form. In *Comanche Station* (1960), Scott plays a man seeking a wife taken by Indians; in *Decision at Sundown* (1957), he is a husband

hunting the man who provoked his wife's suicide; in *The Tall T* (1957), a kidnapped wife becomes the hero's reward when the husband proves unworthy in ordeal; and in *Seven Men From Now* (1956), he is a man hunting down a gang who murdered his wife.

This pattern reaches its height of complexity in John Ford's *The Searchers* (1956), a quest movie in which one of the searchers, Ethan Edwards (John Wayne), seems determined to find, and kill, his niece (Natalie Wood) because she has lived so long with the Comanches. *The Searchers* is torn between community and solitariness, and it seems that Ford himself is moved to confusion by his own story. Ethan Edwards hates Indians and the tainting of his niece that he presumes must have occurred in her marriage to Chief Scar – but the film discovers her lithe and unmarked. Ethan carries her back to the homestead, then turns to slip back into the desert landscape – some force pulling him away from domesticity. Thus racial mixture is cautiously permitted, and the world of women is left in control.

Although there is also a real squaw in *The Searchers*, Look, played by Beulah Archuletta, she is fat and ugly. Not even her death merits any dignity or respect in this resonantly inconsistent picture. As a rule Indian women were as fetching as Natalie Wood – dark actresses in braid and buckskin, such as Jean Peters, fiery and primitive in *Apache* (1954), Sarita Montiel in *Run of the Arrow* (1957) and even Dolores del Rio in *Cheyenne Autumn* (1964).

Portrayals of Indian women that contain any dramatic originality are few. They include Elizabeth Threatt in *The Big Sky* (1952) as a squaw loved by two white men and strong enough to persuade her choice to live with her tribe, and Audrey Hepburn in *The Unforgiven* (1960). The latter, directed by John Huston, is a companion piece to *The Searchers*. They both come from novels written by Alan Le May, but in the Huston film Hepburn is a Kiowa Indian who was taken by a white family.

There are some instances of women in Westerns who are interested in more than running their household. *Gone With the Wind* (1939) has elements of the Western, and Scarlett O'Hara is a belle who matures as a landowner, ready to shoot trespassers. Sometimes even the saloon girl could rise in the world. In *Destry Rides Again* (1939), Marlene Dietrich plays a tempestuous entertainer subdued by cowpoke James Stewart. But in *Rancho Notorious* (1952) she plays a business-woman with a hideaway ranch for outlaws, but now more concerned with security than action.

18

Below: Hannie Caulder (Raquel Welch) scantily prepared to take revenge on her attackers. Bottom: Claudia Cardinale as a 'kidnapped' wife, with Robert Ryan, Woody Strode and Lee Marvin as The Professionals *(1966) hired to save her. Left: Barbara Stanwyck and John Ericson in* Forty Guns – *the bluff is called and the female hostage is shot. Far left and above: Western ladies suffer like Sally (Joan Leslie) in* The Woman They Almost Lynched *(1952); and Tess (Joanne Dru) in* Red River, *with Montgomery Clift*

In Samuel Fuller's *Forty Guns* (1957) a ranching empire is controlled by a woman (Barbara Stanwyck) every bit as confident as a man. In *Cimarron* (1960) the home-building wife, played by Maria Schell, takes over her husband's newspaper when he drifts away, and becomes a pillar of the community. Julie Christie portrays an unsentimental whorehouse proprietress in *McCabe and Mrs Miller* (1971), a movie that admits the true, dismal face of frontier whores – so different from the centre-folds that Pat Garrett (James Coburn) takes to bed in *Pat Garrett and Billy the Kid* (1973).

Joan Crawford as Vienna in *Johnny Guitar* (1954) is entirely commanding. But, like most power-orientated women in Westerns, Vienna has a tender heart beneath her gunslinger's outfit. Possibly even more impressive in this brilliant, outrageous film is Mercedes McCambridge as the leader of a lynch-mob. Virulent and exaggerated, she is still one of the most intriguing female characters in a Western.

There are few women as strong and compelling: the Western has always been short of demanding human confrontations, and so is often stuffed with ritual. The exceptions are therefore all the more remarkable. King Vidor's *Duel in the Sun* (1946), Raoul Walsh's *Pursued* (1947) and Anthony Mann's *The Furies* (1950) are psychological melodramas set in the West, and all from scripts or books by Niven Busch. They study the all-consuming search for love and identity, and they show women free of genre restrictions.

The West seldom has time for more than cursory love stories. But in Anthony Mann's *The Last Frontier* (1955), a blonde Anne Bancroft plays a cavalry officer's wife so drawn to a scout (Victor Mature) that their relationship mirrors the film's conflict between military order and free nature. In *Shane* (1953), Jean Arthur, as the homesteader's wife, cannot own up to her mixed feelings for the nomad gunman; and in Nicholas Ray's *The Lusty Men* (1952), Susan Hayward plays, simultaneously, a determined home-builder and a woman who cannot stop herself loving the battered rodeo veteran played by Robert Mitchum. There are even some Westerns that deserve a place in the history of erotic film: for example, *The Outlaw* (1943), with Jane Russell's cleavage making the most inviting of box canyons; and *Man of the West* (1958), where Julie London, as a saloon singer, has to strip to save the life of a reformed outlaw (Gary Cooper).

Howard Hawks is a director who saw through the limitations of so many genres. And his *Red River* (1948) is about men at last heeding the views of women. The cowboy (John Wayne) leaves his love (Coleen Gray) and she is killed by Indians. Years later he meets Tess Millay (Joanne Dru) who reminds him of his old love, and by winning the heart of his adopted son she then breaks up the supposedly implacable fight between father and son. It is a moment in which a woman finally tells the men to grow up. But this is only a prelude to Angie Dickinson's portrayal of Feathers in *Rio Bravo* (1959) – so perceptive, so muddled, Feathers is a gambling girl but a good woman, articulate, emotional, sensible and sensitive. She is a Western lady who proves herself as both a female and an individual – and thus she is one of the richest women in American films, let alone in Westerns.
DAVID THOMSON

19

Tall in the saddle, honest, quick with a gun but just as likely to burst into song, the B-movie cowboy heroes provided many thrilling hours of screen entertainment. They were kingly figures indeed – worthy of every small boy's adulation

The humble, second-feature B Western is usually dismissed as routine assembly-line product – what denigrators of the form have in mind when they say that all Westerns are the same. To most fans, however, the 'B' stood for 'better' not 'budget' Westerns, and the cowboy stars who appeared in them are worthy of study because sometimes they overcame the limitations of film-making on the cheap to produce works of surprising merit.

Broncho Billy's big break
The first cowboy star was Max Aronson (b. 1882), a Jewish ex-travelling salesman and fashion model from Little Rock, Arkansas, who changed his name to the more suitably Anglo-Saxon Gilbert M. Anderson when he tried to break into pictures. In 1903 Anderson persuaded Edwin S. Porter, who was casting for his film *The Great Train Robbery* (1903), that he was an expert horseman (in fact, he only learned to ride two years later). Anderson played several roles in the movie – a victim of the holdup, a member of the posse and one of the outlaws it was chasing. In 1910 Anderson first appeared as Broncho Billy, the character who was to make him a pioneer of the star system in films like *Broncho Billy's Redemption* (1910). The good-badman hero he generally played was an enormous success and by the time Anderson's career as Broncho Billy bit the dust in 1918 (due to the competition from

features), he had acted in nearly four hundred shorts. In his prime Anderson churned out Westerns for his company Essanay at the rate of one a week, earning $125,000 a year as producer, director and star. In 1957 he was plucked from obscurity to receive an Oscar for 'contributions to the development of motion pictures as entertainment'. He died in 1971.

Above: a tinted frame from an unidentified film shows Broncho Billy Anderson in big trouble. Right: publicity portrait of Roy Rogers and Trigger from 1945. Below: William S. Hart as The Gun Fighter *(1917) who is reformed by a pretty milliner but dies rescuing her from an outlaw. Below, far right: an admiring glance for Tom Mix as the well-dressed* Son of the Golden West *(1928)*

Hart in the right place
Broncho Billy Anderson's mantle as leading Western star passed during the mid-1910s to William S. Hart (b. 1870), a dour-faced ex-Broadway classical actor (hence the legend that the 'S' stood for Shakespeare – actually his middle name was Surrey). Hailing from Newburgh, New York State, Hart had travelled extensively in the West as a young man and developed an abiding love for its folklore and history. He was already 44 years old when in 1914 he began making two-reel Westerns for his friend the director and producer Thomas H. Ince, whose Inceville studio specialized in Westerns. By 1916 Hart was producing, directing and starring in his own feature-length Westerns, the best known of which are *Hell's Hinges* and *The Aryan* (both 1916). In 1917 he followed Ince from the Triangle Film Corporation to Paramount where he made numerous large-budget films, including his greatest box-office hit *The Toll Gate* (1920) and *Wild Bill Hickok* (1923).

Hart's Westerns are noted for their supposedly stark realism and unglamorized portrait of the Old West. In fact, the realism is only superficial, confined to the costumes, sets and physical paraphernalia. Hart's favourite role, like Anderson's, was the good-badman, redeemed by a woman, child or clergyman. The plots of his films are standard Victorian melodrama in Western guise. However, they are sometimes downbeat and pessimistic, a

KINGS OF THE

WILD FRONTIER

and a keen eye for publicity. Mix's studio biography put out the legend that he was the son of a cavalry officer, and had seen action in the Spanish-American War, the Philippine Insurrection, the Boxer Rebellion in China and the Boer War. He was also said to have been a deputy marshal in Oklahoma and a Texas Ranger. In fact, his father was a lumberman, and although Tom had served in the US Artillery he had been listed as a deserter in 1902. But he was a skilled horseman, had briefly joined the Texas Rangers, and from 1906 worked for Wild West shows, winning several championships. It was as a rodeo rider that he was discovered by the Selig company for whom he made over a hundred Western shorts between 1909 and 1917, most of them heavily laced with folksy humour. His career really took off when he joined Fox in 1917 and began a series of features starting with *The Heart of Texas Ryan* and including *Just Tony* (1922), a great success built around his trusty steed, as well as *Riders of the Purple Sage* (1925) and the appropriately titled *King Cowboy* (1928). With the coming of sound, Mix returned to rodeo touring for some years. Between 1932 and 1934, he made a Western series for Universal which failed to restore his former screen dominance, although it included several very successful entries like *My Pal, the King*, co-starring the young Mickey Rooney, *Destry Rides Again* and *Riders of Death Valley* (all 1932).

After the Mascot serial *The Miracle Rider* (1935), which grossed over a million dollars, Mix retired from the screen. On October 12, 1940, wearing a fancy outfit complete with a diamond-studded belt-buckle and a white ten-gallon hat, he crashed his custom-built roadster while speeding across Arizona. His funeral, with Rudy Vallee crooning 'Empty Saddles' to a star-studded gathering, was as much a show-business spectacle as his life had been.

opposed to the lighter-hearted escapism of the films starring Tom Mix who by the early twenties was overtaking Hart in popularity. Quarrelling with Paramount over their pressure to lighten the tone of his films, Hart moved to United Artists as an independent producer, where in 1925 he completed his masterpiece *Tumbleweeds*, a spectacular depiction of land-rush days. Although *Tumbleweeds* was a success critically and at the box-office, Hart felt United Artists had not realized its full potential through negligent distribution and sued them. He won over $250,000 in damages but his career in films was ruined and he retired to his ranch where he died in 1946.

Another Western star to work with Thomas H. Ince was John Ford's older brother Francis (1882–1953), who starred in *Custer's Last Raid* (1912). He directed and acted in numerous serials and shorts for Universal, but his career waned in the sound era and he ended up taking character roles in his brother's films.

Hits for Mix

In the Twenties, Western series developed mostly as escapist entertainment. The emphasis was on spectacular stunts, action and fun provided by the 'Big Five' cowboy stars of the period: Tom Mix, Buck Jones, Ken Maynard, Tim McCoy and Hoot Gibson.

Tom Mix (b. 1881) was the first to glamorize the screen image of the cowboy, with gaudy, inauthentic, impractical outfits,

Left: a 1937 Western with Buck Jones as secret agent Alamo Bowie. Above: Jack (Tim McCoy) and his girl (Allene Ray) learn that The Indians Are Coming. Below: a 1933 star vehicle for Ken Maynard. Bottom: Hoot Gibson (right) in The Texas Streak (1926)

Along came Jones

Closely following Mix in popularity in the Twenties was Buck Jones (b. 1889), who became the leading cowboy star of the talkies. Jones was the acme of the cowboy hero, and his performances embodied the dignity and quiet determination that is the quintessential image of the screen Westerner, blended with an appealing touch of humour. Like Mix, Jones had been an expert rider from childhood, but his off-screen exploits fully lived up to his film persona. Joining the US Cavalry at the age of 17, Jones saw action in Mexico and the Philippines. He followed this with a career in Wild West shows that led to stunt-work in Hollywood in 1917. By 1919 he was starring in

Westerns, and reached the height of his popularity in the early Thirties in his Columbia and Universal series, with films like *Shadow Ranch* (1930) and *The Crimson Trail* (1935). In the late Thirties his popularity waned, but he was restored to success when Monogram teamed him with Tim McCoy in the Rough Riders series in 1941. In December 1942, while on a tour selling War Bonds, Buck Jones died a hero's death when he returned repeatedly to rescue people trapped in a nightclub fire that eventually overcame him.

The real McCoy

Buck Jones' fellow Rough Rider Tim McCoy (b. 1891) also lived up to his cowboy hero image

off-screen. McCoy was an expert on Indian customs and languages, and following his discharge from military service in World War I with the rank of Lieutenant-Colonel, he became Indian Agent for a Sioux reservation in Wyoming. His entry into films was as co-ordinator of Indian extras for the director James Cruze on *The Covered Wagon* (1923). In 1925 he starred in the only Western series ever made at MGM, and some of its films – including *War Paint* (1926), *Winners of the Wilderness* and *California* (both 1927) – were far more ambitious affairs than most series Westerns. McCoy later starred in the first sound serial *The Indians Are Coming* for Universal in 1930, and made a successful series for Columbia. Like Buck Jones, his popularity slipped in the late Thirties and he appeared for several Poverty Row Independents before being restored to the Western front rank in the Rough Riders series. After military service during World War II, Colonel McCoy retired to his ranch where he died in 1978, aged 87.

Two rode together

The other two of the silent 'Big Five' Western stars, Ken Maynard (b. 1895) and Hoot Gibson (b. 1892), also finished their careers teamed up in a Monogram series of the early Forties – The Trail Blazers. Both had entered films via rodeo. Maynard had been a trick rider with Buffalo Bill's Wild West Show. Gibson won the 1912 title of 'World's All-Around Champion Cowboy'. Both rose to prominence as Western stars in the Twenties, Gibson being noted for his breezy style, emphasizing comedy over action, while Maynard and his horse Tarzan rode through many stunt-filled spectaculars at First National which were plundered for stock-footage for years afterwards. Gibson and Maynard survived the transition to sound for a few years, and Maynard is credited with the introduction of songs into Westerns. Both Maynard and Gibson fared badly after the mid-Thirties, despite their teaming as The Trail Blazers. Maynard passed into alcoholic decline and poverty, dying of malnutrition in a rented

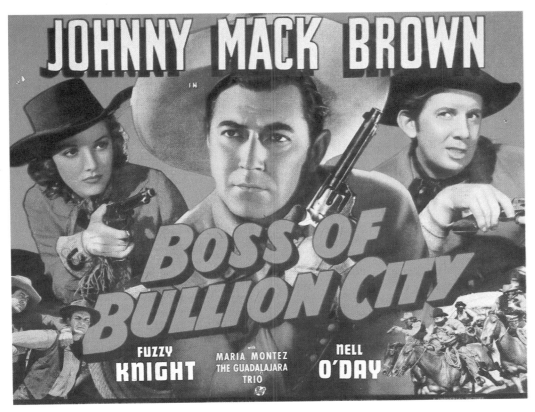

Above: a 1937 tale of corrupt lawmen starred Johnny Mack Brown as the newspaper boss who restores order to Bullion City. Below left: Fred Thomson (in real life a former pastor) and Silver King in Jesse James

trailer at the age of 77 in 1973. Gibson retired after the war, apart from a few cameo roles, and died in 1962.

Trails gone astray

Behind the 'Big Five' there were numerous other important silent B-Western stars. Two of the most successful at the time, Art Acord and Fred Thomson, are little known today. Acord (b. 1890) was another former rodeo star, who became Universal's top cowboy of the Twenties, but his career did not survive the transition to sound. He became an unsuccessful bootlegger and gambler, and in 1931 was found dead from cyanide poisoning in a Mexican hotel. Thomson's career as a cowboy

star lasted only five years from 1923 until his untimely death of pneumonia in 1928 aged 38. His stuntwork and acrobatics on his horse Silver King in such FBO vehicles as *Jesse James* (1927) and *Kit Carson* (1928) are legendary.

Harry Carey (b. 1878) began in D. W. Griffith's films in 1909, and his first starring Westerns were directed by John Ford. He had a great success as *Trader Horn* in 1931, but then appeared mainly in character roles, often for Ford, until his death in 1947. Granite-faced Jack Holt (1888–1951) starred in many successful Westerns of Zane Grey stories in the Twenties, as well as in non-Westerns. By the mid-Thirties he was mainly seen in character roles. His son Tim (1918–73) and daughter Jennifer (b. 1920) starred in numerous Forties B-Western series. Tom Tyler (1903–54) and Bob Steele (b. 1906) were silent Western stars who continued into the sound era. They both also made successful appearances in non-Western parts, Tyler in *The Adventures of Captain Marvel* (1941), and Steele in *Of Mice and Men* (1939) and *The Big Sleep* (1946), among others. Other silent Western stars – including Lane Chandler (1899–1972), Wally Wales (b. 1895), Rex Lease (1901–66) and Jack Perrin (1896–1967) – survived into the sound era mainly in supporting roles, or, like Yakima Canutt (b. 1895), the greatest stuntman of them all, as doubles.

The leading B-Western newcomers of the early Thirties all began in the big-time. Former champion athlete George O'Brien (b. 1900), son of a San Francisco police chief, had starred in two silent classics, John Ford's *The Iron Horse* (1924) and F. W. Murnau's *Sunrise* (1927). But from 1930 until his retirement in 1940 he appeared only in series Westerns, first for Fox, then RKO. John Wayne's first starring role was

in Raoul Walsh's *The Big Trail* (1930), but the film was not a success and Wayne starred throughout the Thirties in numerous serials and B Westerns before returning to the top in *Stagecoach* (1939). He is the only B-Western star ever to achieve true superstar status. Johnny Mack Brown (1904–74), the other B-Western newcomer of the early Thirties, had begun his career as a non-Western lead for MGM in the late Twenties, and in the early sound years starred in big-budget productions such as King Vidor's *Billy the Kid* (1930). But by 1933 his stock was reduced to starring in a Mascot serial *Fighting With Kit Carson*, and thereafter he appeared in B-Western series for Republic, Universal and Monogram, right up to 1953.

Rhythms of the range
In 1935 the B Western was revolutionized when Gene Autry starred in the Mascot serial *The Phantom Empire*, a curious hybrid of science-fiction and cowboy-adventure, and his first Republic feature *Tumbling Tumbleweeds*. Guitars joined guns as the cowboy's tools of the trade, and the musical Western was born. It took to extremes the fantasy world of the B Western as modern gadgets like cars, planes, even U-boats were mixed anachronistically with the six-guns, sagebrush and songs of the saddle.

Autry's phenomenal success stimulated many imitators in the Thirties, including Tex Ritter (1905–74), Dick Foran (b. 1910), Smith Ballew (b. 1911), Fred Scott (b. 1902), Bob Baker (1914–75), James Newill (b. 1911), George Houston (1898–1944) and Jack Randall (1907–45), and in the Forties such sage-brush warblers as Eddie Dean (b. 1910), Jimmy Wakely (b. 1914), Rex Allen (b. 1922) and Monte Hale (b. 1921). But Autry's only real rival was a fresh-faced kid called Leonard Slye (b. 1912) from Duck Run, Ohio, who won the accolade 'King of the Cowboys' in the Forties under the name Roy Rogers.

Rogers had been groomed by Republic as a means of disciplining their leading Western star, and when Autry joined the Air Force in World War II the studio elevated Rogers as his

successor. Both Rogers and Autry survived at the top until the demise of the B Western in the early Fifties and then made highly lucrative television series.

Hoppy in the saddle
Despite the prominence of the musical Western after 1935, several important new non-singing cowboy stars appeared. Foremost among these was William Boyd (1898–1972), who had starred in a number of Cecil B. DeMille's silent films, including *The Volga Boatman* (1926). Prematurely grey, fallen on hard times, and unable to ride, Boyd was an unlikely Western lead. But he landed the plum part of Hopalong Cassidy in 1935, and began one of the most

Above: Texas Ranger Hopalong Cassidy (William Boyd) knocks out Drago (a young Robert Mitchum) in Riders of the Deadline *(1944). Below: publicity portrait of Gene Autry, taken at Columbia in the late Forties*

successful and longest running of all Western series. When Hopalong Cassidy's cinematic popularity faded, Boyd was able to make a successful transition to television, becoming the white-haired, moralizing patriarch to a new generation of kids. Other non-singing cowboys who achieved some fame in the Forties as action stars included Gordon 'Wild Bill' Elliott (1904–65), with his soft-spoken catchphrase, 'I'm a peaceable man', the inevitable prelude to his beating the hell out of the heavies; Allan 'Rocky' Lane (1904–73); Charles Starrett (b. 1903), best known as 'the Durango Kid'; Tim Holt; Don 'Red' Barry (1912–80); Ray 'Crash' Corrigan (1907–76); 'Sunset' Carson (b. 1925); Rod Cameron (b. 1912); Al 'Lash' LaRue (b. 1917); 'Whip' Wilson (1919–64); Bob Livingston (b. 1908); and the former Warner Brothers star Wayne Morris (1914–59), who had the dubious distinction of making the very last series B Western, Allied Artists' *Two Guns and a Badge* (1954).

Good guys and bad
The iconography of the B Western was fixed from the days of Tom Mix. The hero was clean and had a white hat and horse, while the villain sported stubble, a moustache and a paunch. A few films strove for novelty by reversing the standard dress: Tim McCoy and Lash LaRue wore black, while the Lone Ranger and Durango Kid movies tried the gimmick of a masked hero.

The B Western's ideology is best described as populist rather than straightforwardly conservative. The villain is almost invariably a banker or mayor with a respectable front. His image reflects all the suspicion and hostility with which poor, rural, mainly Southern audiences (who were the genre's prime consumers) regarded urban financiers and politicians.

The B Western died in 1954, victim of rising costs, television competition, and the changing tastes of audiences, which made never-never land escapism unpalatable. But the concerns and conventions pioneered by the form continued to influence the large-budget Western for many years. ROBERT REINER

Lonesome trail

After a big-guns opening to the sound era, Westerns fell from popularity in the Thirties until 1939's bumper crop of cowboy pictures proved that old genres never die

In the Western actions usually spoke louder than 'words', but when the sound revolution occurred the craze was for films with plenty of dialogue – comedies and musicals. So in the early days of talkies the immediate outlook for the Western was bleak. To make matters worse the sound engineers claimed that recording outdoors would be difficult, if not impossible.

In the ensuing uncertainty, the big Western stars of the silent cinema – Tom Mix, Ken Maynard, Tim McCoy – were dropped by their studios. Only Universal persevered, pumping out more of its Hoot Gibson Westerns and later snapping up Maynard and McCoy. But it was the director Raoul Walsh and the crew of *In Old Arizona* (1929) who quashed any reservations about applying sound to outdoor subjects.

The film was a modest Cisco Kid drama based on a story by O. Henry with a typical twist in which the Kid neatly revenges himself on a double-crossing señorita and outwits the law at the same time. The incidental sounds were laid on somewhat heavily, but audiences were thrilled at the clear recording of lips being smacked after a character had swallowed a drink, of eggs and bacon frying, and of horses' hoofs fading away as riders departed. There was also a zestful performance by Warner Baxter as the laughing bandit who serenaded his faithless señorita with the song 'My Tonia'. Baxter won the Academy Award in 1929 for Best Actor and *In Old Arizona* was the smash hit that restored

Westerns to favour.

The same year saw Victor Fleming's painstaking screen version of the thrice-filmed story *The Virginian* (1929) in which Gary Cooper made a suitably laconic hero forced to hang the friend who has turned cattle-rustler.

The Western was so strong a box-office prospect that by 1930 it was seen as a suitable candidate for wide-screen experimentation. MGM made *Billy the Kid* (1930) which was shot in the 70mm Realife process; Fox released its epic *The Big Trail* (1930) which ran 158 minutes in its Fox Grandeur version and 125 minutes in the standard 35mm version (both were shot simultaneously). Warners contributed *The Lash* (1930), a romantic adventure set in the California of the 1850s with Richard Barthelmess as a Spanish nobleman who turns bandit in order to overthrow a crooked American land commissioner. This movie was released in yet another wide-screen process: 65mm Vitascope.

Despite the resurgence of interest in Westerns, these three films flopped at the box-office owing to resistance on the part of exhibitors to the cost of installing wide-screen systems in their cinemas. Experimentation with 65mm and 70mm film gauges had raised the production cost enormously, and because of their failure the Western was once again brought into disrepute as far as the big producers were concerned.

Billy the Kid (dir. King Vidor) was a straightforward, slow, austere account of the young outlaw's

Top: William S. Hart, the foremost star of silent Westerns, hands over to the talkie star, John Mack Brown. The gun used for this historic occasion is reputed to have belonged to the real-life outlaw Billy the Kid. Left: Indian chiefs survey the range in Raoul Walsh's The Big Trail

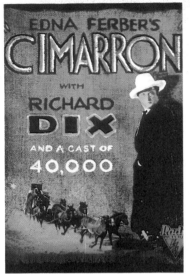

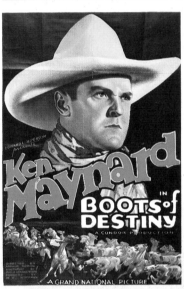

Top: Cimarron *portrayed the life
of an Oklahoma family between
1890 and 1915. Above: Ken
Maynard, an early cowboy star,
continued well into the Thirties in
B pictures like this 1938 Western.
Below: wagons roll westwards in*
The Big Trail

life, using the Grand Canyon for its locations. Although the film altered the facts by allowing a reformed Billy to go off with his girl at the end, the high death count up to that point set a harsh tone that did not appeal to audiences. John Mack Brown played Billy but it was not a role that suited him and he was to gain more charisma later in the decade as a star of series Westerns.

The Big Trail (dir. Raoul Walsh) was made to celebrate the centenary of a pioneering wagon-train journey that had set out from Independence, Missouri. The movie was shot under conditions almost as gruelling as those endured by the original travellers. It contained spectacular scenes of a buffalo hunt, a massive Indian attack on a circle of wagons, the fording of a swollen river and the lowering of cattle and wagons down a sheer cliff-face, in settings ranging from rainstorms and blizzards to desert heat. Unfortunately the human-interest was feeble and the casting of the unknown John Wayne as the wagon-train scout was a gamble that did not pay off at the box-office, although Wayne acquitted himself well. The final image fittingly celebrates the might of nature – the film's most impressive theme – as Wayne strides out of frame to be reunited with the heroine (Marguerite Churchill) and the camera tilts upwards to take in the towering trees of the forest setting.

The only Western ever to win the Academy Award for the year's Best Picture was *Cimarron* (1931). But this was more than a Western: based on one of Edna Ferber's vast, sprawling, generation-spanning sagas, it was an epic about the development of Oklahoma. It began with a spectacular reconstruction of the Cherokee Strip land-rush and continued through to the oil boom of the twentieth century. The success of *Cimarron* spawned such imitations as *The Conquerors* (1932) with the same star, Richard Dix, and *Secrets* (1933), with Mary Pickford and Leslie Howard. The latter film was the only main feature Western among the sixty or so released in 1933.

Before the genre went into the wilderness of the B

movie there was one notable, medium-scale Western, *Law and Order* (dir. Edward Cahn, 1932) which drew heavily on the story of Wyatt Earp bringing law to Tombstone and of the gunfight at the OK Corral. Walter Huston brought his usual authority to the central role and the script was written in part by his son John Huston. Cahn's direction provided some powerful sequences as, for example, the coverage of a lynch mob's arrival on horseback, townsfolk thronging the balconies around the jail-house, then edging forward slightly (the camera edging with them) to press in on Huston who is waiting on the steps outside. Cahn composed a striking finale to the film, shooting the march towards the final showdown with his camera set low, tracking backwards in front of Huston and his men as they stride purposefully forward.

After this production, however, it was left to the B picture units and the Poverty Row studios to keep the Western alive, though usually in the series format. In 1935, however, minor Westerns doubled in number in response to public demand, and two important developments in the genre occurred. First there was the arrival of Gene Autry, a former radio singer, who made his debut as a singing cowboy in the serial *The Phantom Empire* and the feature *Tumbling Tumbleweeds* (both 1935). Songs and comedy became major ingredients in Autry's work and his bland easy-going personality set the tone for the relaxed quality of his films which non-metropolitan audiences found especially to their liking. His stories were set in a fantasy land where contemporary and period details merged – aircraft, for example, could co-exist comfortably with old-fashioned stagecoaches.

The second key development was the Hopalong Cassidy series starring William Boyd as the blond knight of the range. Boyd was an accomplished performer who could handle action as ably as he could deliver lines; responding to a query about his guns in *Bar 20 Rides Again* (1935), he says, 'I just wear them to keep my legs warm'. The Hopalong Cassidy series was a success and encouraged Para-

mount, who had distributed it, to venture into big Westerns again.

So in 1936 King Vidor made *The Texas Rangers* with Fred MacMurray as the former stagecoach robber who joins the lawmen and brings an old partner (played by Lloyd Nolan) to justice. More significant, however, was Cecil B. DeMille's *The Plainsman* (1936) a lavish pot-pourri that starred Gary Cooper as Wild Bill Hickok, Jean Arthur as Calamity Jane, James Ellison as Buffalo Bill, John Miljan as Custer and Frank McGlynn Sr as Abraham Lincoln. Its robust action scenes, filmed by the second-unit director Arthur Rosson, blended awkwardly with studio close-ups of the stars firing at back-projections of marauding Indians. There were also moments of light relief as, for example, when a bullet was fired into a water-keg to provide a stream of water for a man lying wounded underneath – but at least DeMille insisted on a factual conclusion with Hickok being shot in the back and dying. Paramount followed this slice of comic-strip history with Frank Lloyd's static *Wells Fargo* (1937), starring Joel McCrea, and James Hogan's livelier *The Texans* (1938), with Randolph Scott, Joan Bennett and Walter Brennan.

Surprisingly, although three-strip Technicolor was being used by Paramount and other studios on outdoor subjects it was not used in Westerns until *Jesse James* (1939), although a number of Warners' outdoor films – *God's Country and the Woman* (1936), *Gold is Where You Find it* and *Heart of the North* (both 1938) – were almost Westerns. Then two films, Fox's *Jesse James* and Paramount's DeMille extravaganza *Union Pacific* (1939) triggered a great Western boom; the trade paper *Variety* noted the trend early in 1939.

'Out of Hollywood from now until the end of the present production year in midsummer, will flow the rootin', tootin', shootin'est, bowie-knife wielding bunch of ride 'em cowboy, major budget Westerns the picture business has witnessed in a decade. Some $15,000,000 worth of shooting, scalping, train and stagecoach robbing, hypoed with

gentle love, mad brawls for the protection of honour and "curse you, Jack Dalton" villains has been budgeted.'

Variety's explanation for the revival of the genre was the cyclical nature of the business and the copy-cat techniques of the studios; all of them were making Westerns for fear of being left out of a forthcoming box-office bonanza. But other factors may have come into play. *Variety*'s report of a 'surge of Americanism' in film subject-matter was only to be expected as the European situation worsened. Key foreign markets were threatened or already lost, and films with strong domestic appeal made sense at the box-office.

Furthermore, cinema attendance figures in the United States had become static despite the rise in population and the studios were consequently making changes in film content in the hope of building new audiences.

One picture has come to stand out from all the rest in the bumper crop of 1939: *Stagecoach*. It was John Ford's first Western since *Three Bad Men* (1926) but was not an outstanding success commercially. *Variety* announced:

'*Stagecoach* at the box-office has not sustained the enthusiastic reviews it received from the press. Lack of strong names in the cast and a trite title are the reasons given for the *Stagecoach* fade.'

But the praise heaped on the film and the evident skill of Ford's direction did have a strong influence on other film-makers: it made the Western a respectable subject for quality films. If the year had not been dominated by *Gone With the Wind*, the film would have won more Oscars than the two it did.

In a dramatic sense *Stagecoach* was not essentially a Western – its carefully assorted band of passengers could have been assembled in any setting and exposed to an equivalent danger to show their reaction under stress. And almost all the scenes involving the leading players were filmed in the studio. But besides John Ford's inimitable use of Monument Valley and his striking chase sequence across salt flats, there was his masterful treatment

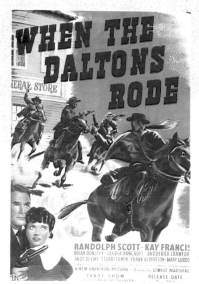

Top: Randolph Scott, Kay Francis, Brian Donlevy and Andy Devine were among the familiar names in popular Westerns; here they were teamed in a version of the Daltons legend. Above: the singing cowboy Gene Autry made his feature-film debut in the Western with songs, Tumbling Tumbleweeds

Top: on location with The Texans. *The large circular disc is designed to reflect sunlight on the couple in the buckboard – Joan Bennett and Robert Cummings. Top right: Ronald Reagan and Errol Flynn prepare to shoot it out in* Santa Fe Trail. *Above: Wyler's prestige Western based on the life of Judge Roy Bean. Below: Tyrone Power in* Jesse James

of the traditional gunfight on main street. Moreover the dynamic performance of John Wayne, in such moments as the halting of the runaway stage or when he dives to the ground to fire on his opponents in the climactic shoot-out, assured the actor of front-rank stardom that had eluded him since *The Big Trail*.

Both *Jesse James* and *Dodge City* (1939) eclipsed *Stagecoach* in box-office terms; they had top stars and were in Technicolor. *The Oklahoma Kid* (1939) was another success. James Cagney wore a ten-gallon hat and brought his city-slicker mannerisms to the role of the Robin Hood of Oklahoma, and Humphrey Bogart, dressed in black from tip to toe, played the dastardly villain, but the movie was tongue-in-cheek and deserved its success. *Jesse James* was a romanticized depiction of the celebrated outlaw's life with sympathetic portrayals from both Tyrone Power as Jesse and Henry Fonda as his brother Frank; the two of them take up robbery only after the railroad's representative (played by Brian Donlevy) has burnt down the family farm and killed their mother. Jesse's actual death (he was shot in the back) was retained but the newspaper editor, acting as chorus or commentator, gave the film an upbeat ending eulogizing Jesse:

'We ain't ashamed of him – I don't think even America is ashamed of Jesse James. Maybe it was because he was bold and lawless like all of us like to be sometimes, maybe it's because we understand a little that he wasn't altogether to blame for what his times made him . . .'

The cue had been given for the Old West's other badmen to be covered in Hollywood whitewash. MGM remade *Billy the Kid* (1941) with Robert Taylor; Gene Tierney appeared as the notorious *Belle Starr* (1941) and Universal told of *When the Daltons Rode* (1940).

In contrast *Dodge City* was merely an actionful Western with Errol Flynn dispensing the heroics to a zestful score by Max Steiner. Michael Curtiz's direction displayed its usual panache but the script by Robert Buckner was rather weak. The same combination of star, composer and director were brought in to liven up two more Buckner screenplays: *Virginia City* and *Santa Fe Trail* (both 1940).

DeMille's *Union Pacific* was the epic story of the construction of the first transcontinental railway. No expense was spared to give the film an authentic look: the top track-laying crew of the actual Union Pacific company was recruited to perform in front of the cameras, and there was a spectacular Indian attack on a moving train, staged by Arthur Rosson. The main plot featured Joel McCrea as the overseer fighting saboteurs (led by Brian Donlevy, the period's most hard-working screen villain) while avenging the death of a friend at the same time. The narrative was stronger than that of *The Plainsman* and DeMille gained some inspiration from John Ford's *The Iron Horse* (1924) which had the same historical background.

Even Republic, the leading source of B Westerns, with its singing cowboys Gene Autry and Roy Rogers, decided the time was right to move up-market. Borrowing a star, Richard Dix, a director, George Nichols Jr, and a supporting actress, Joan Fontaine, they made *Man of Conquest* (1939), the story of the pioneer Sam Houston, that culminated in a rousing reconstruction of the battle of San Jacinto. So contagious was the fever for big Westerns that even the 'quality film' specialist Sam Goldwyn succumbed and hired William Wyler to make *The Westerner* (1940), Goldwyn's second (and last) horse opera. The film was a cleverly written account of the relationship between an honest cowpoke (played by Gary Cooper) and the wily Judge Roy Bean (Walter Brennan in an Oscar-winning portrayal).

At the turn of the decade the Western was in such strong shape that it even encouraged the satirical treatment of George Marshall's *Destry Rides Again* (1939), a light-hearted re-working of a Max Brand story that had been filmed straight in 1927 as Tom Mix's first sound film. James Stewart played the apparently naive and helpless Destry who helps clean up a town while Marlene Dietrich was the saloon singer who fell for his good looks and innocent charm.

The astonishing recovery of the genre put it back on its feet for good, but the excitement and vitality of the Westerns of the 1939–41 period was only short-lived.

ALLEN EYLES

How John Ford's West was Won

The heroes of John Ford's films are the frontiersmen, pioneers and peacemakers who dedicated themselves to the founding of the homes and communities that make up America. Ford's vision is a folk vision: a celebration of the ideals that sent wagon trains of settlers westwards in search of freedom and opportunity, but couched in the homeliest of terms – where a dance or a gathering round a graveside speaks volumes more than the dramatic battles and gunfights that were also waged in the winning of the West

Above: Stagecoach, *in which John Ford (inset) first made use of the spectacular mesas of Monument Valley, Utah. The film itself was a landmark in the career of one of the most respected directors in world cinema. Ford (1895–1973) directed his first feature,* Tornado, *in 1917. Born Sean Aloysius O'Feeney, thirteenth child of Irish immigrant parents, in Maine, he had come to Hollywood after failing to get into naval college. He worked his way up as prop man, stunt man and actor*

By the end of the Thirties John Ford already had a hundred films to his name. Whereas a lesser director would have probably burned himself out, the best years for Ford were still ahead. His 'golden age' spanned nearly three decades. It began in 1939 with two films, *Stagecoach* and *Young Mr Lincoln*, and encompassed along the way such milestones as *She Wore a Yellow Ribbon* (1949), *Wagonmaster* (1950) and *The Searchers* (1956). These films are packed with unforgettable sequences and images: the young Lincoln (Henry Fonda) climbing a hill in a storm; Nathan Brittles (John Wayne), the old cavalry captain in *She*

Wore a Yellow Ribbon, riding out of the fort for a final mission and furtively shielding his face from the sun, or Brittles going to his wife's grave in the evening to 'talk' to her. There is the moment when the showgirl Denver (Joanne Dru) flashes a mysterious look at the wagon-train leader Travis (Ben Johnson) in *Wagonmaster*; or when Ethan (Wayne) lifts up and cradles the niece (Natalie Wood) he has sought to kill in *The Searchers*, understanding in those few instants the uselessness of his hatred; or Frank Skeffington (Spencer Tracy) returning home alone after failing to be re-elected as the mayor in *The Last Hurrah* (1958). These

sublime moments in Ford's films reveal more than a thousand critical post-mortems that his art is above all meditative – one might even say symphonic.

The contemplative nature in Ford has rarely been understood. In France, for example, his Westerns have been promoted with pompous phrases like 'heroic charge', 'hellish pursuit' and 'fantastic journey' which suggest that the films somehow belong to the epic genre. Nothing is further from the essence of these fundamentally peaceful works of art. And although Voltaire's assertion that 'Epic authors had to choose a hero whose name alone

Above: Judge Billy Priest (Will Rogers) and other veterans of the Civil War evoke nostalgia for the Confederate States in Judge Priest *(1934). Ford remade the film as* The Sun Shines Bright *in 1953*

would impress itself on the reader' can be applied to certain Ford films like *Young Mr Lincoln* (a splendid evocation of the youth of the American president), it is certainly not applicable to most of his work, including the Westerns. In *My Darling Clementine* (1946), that legendary hero Wyatt Earp (Henry Fonda) is reduced to everyday dimensions; he has no exalted status.

A man's gotta do . . .

It is interesting to compare the socially minded motivation of the typical Ford hero with the personal motivation of the classic Western hero. The classic Western is chiefly built around a ruggedly individualistic vision of the world: Allan Dwan's *Silver Lode* (1954), with John Payne as a man trying to clear his name, and King Vidor's *Man Without a Star* (1955), with Kirk Douglas as a drifter motivated by revenge, are perhaps the most extreme examples of this. Strong feelings, often of physical or psychological violence, predominate; there is hatred, vengeance, rebellion and conquest. A cowboy is usually out to avenge his brother, his friend or his own honour; an outlaw tries to escape from his past; a gunfighter follows his will to kill; a man needs to prove he is not a coward or has to overcome the devil within himself. In short, the genre draws its dramatic force from a few powerful ideas: a confrontation, an opposition, a tearing away. From the films of Raoul Walsh to those of Delmer Daves, Western heroes pitch themselves into a battle by their own free choice. And it is a battle that will allow them to accomplish their purpose – but from which, if they survive, they will emerge permanently scarred. Even if there are no horseback chases or bloody shoot-outs, the dramaturgy of the classic Western is precisely structured and depends on a number of climactic moments.

With Ford, however, the essential motivation is looser, more attenuated, and rarely drawn around an individual emotion or a negative, destructive driving force like vengeance. What predominates at the heart of his Westerns are journeys and wanderings: the slow odyssey of a wagon train, the patrolling of a group of cavalrymen, the crossing of a desert by a stagecoach, or by a group of bandits on the run. Ultimately his films are all odysseys of groups – the stage passengers in *Stagecoach* (1939), farmers and their families escaping from the Oklahoma Dust Bowl in *The Grapes of Wrath* (1940), cavalrymen out on missions in *Fort Apache* (1948), *She Wore a Yellow Ribbon*, *Rio Grande* (1950) and *The Horse Soldiers* (1959), the Mormon settlers in *Wagonmaster*, Ethan and Martin Pawley (Jeffrey Hunter) searching for Debbie in *The Searchers*. Each group consists of several people who either belong to the same walk of life, or are brought together and bound by the same collective purpose. Ford is only interested in personal

problems in so far as they overlap those of society at large; whereas in Howard Hawks' Westerns, for example, adventure remains the right of the individual and only concerns society by chance or accident. In Hawks' *Rio Bravo* (1959) the sheriff (John Wayne) refuses the help offered to him; Ford's Wyatt Earp, however, accepts it immediately. It is a fundamental difference: the first sheriff seeks to fulfil himself through his duty, the second thinks primarily about helping those around him.

. . . what a man's gotta do

At the same time Ford frequently shows us the dissensions and disagreements that divide communities, and his heroes act only in relation to the environment they live in. It is that environment that provides their task – a duty to fulfil for the good of the community; any personal vendettas are usually subjugated to the communal cause. The notion of having a task or a mission takes precedence over all personal considerations. This is especially true of *Rio Grande* in which Captain Kirby Yorke (John Wayne) puts his duty as a soldier before his marriage and family; and in *The Sun Shines Bright* (1953), in which an old Southern judge (Charles Winninger) risks his reputation in

Most of Ford's films are about men working for a common cause and sharing the hardships incurred. Above: John Qualen, Ward Bond, Jack Pennick, John Wayne and Thomas Mitchell toil on the sea in The Long Voyage Home. *Below: Welsh miners enduring a pit disaster in* How Green Was My Valley, *with Walter Pidgeon and Oscar-winner Donald Crisp*

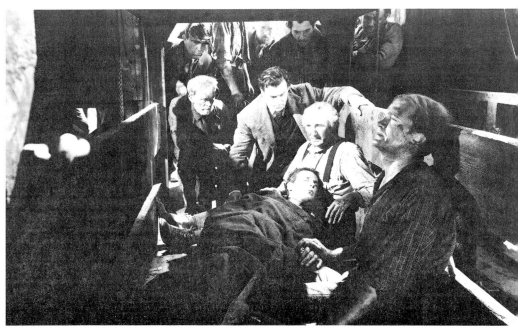

evokes it briefly and objectively, without any indulgence or lyricism; the swift shoot-out at the OK Corral in *My Darling Clementine* and the killing off of the outlaws who threaten the settlers in *Wagonmaster* are good examples.

Even the adventures themselves are non-violent in the way they progress; they are unfolded for us in a rhythm that is at once casual yet majestic. In telling a story Ford takes his time and works like a painter, rather than a strategist or a theoretician.

The true Ford hero has no need to use violence to prove himself. He simply does it, carried along by the collective ideal that leaves no space in his mind for doubt. Perhaps Ford's real heroes are the communities themselves: the unknown soldiers bringing peace to the West; the pioneers who are crossing the country to build new states; the inhabitants of

The story of Ford's films is a great saga of agrarian life: claiming or reclaiming, cultivating and enlarging territorial possessions.

Accordingly Ford's heroes take their character from the peasant, whatever their social origins. Heroes may be Irish peasants, farmers, Welsh miners, soldiers, whatever. In Ford's eyes the soldiers who run a territory in *She Wore a Yellow Ribbon* are involved in the same struggle as the Joad family in *The Grapes of Wrath*. And although the different communities in Ford's films are closed communities governed by their own rules, they are similar in that they share not only the struggles of life but its simple pleasures, too, like a dance, as in *Fort Apache* and *My Darling Clementine*.

The notion of possession accounts for Ford's passion for ceremonies. Celebrations, drunken festivities, dances, even funerals are the tan-

rder to rescue a black boy from being lynched. n *My Darling Clementine* Wyatt Earp's vengence on the Clantons for the killing of his rother is given much less importance than he dance in front of the church and the hakespearian monologues of the travelling howman (Alan Mowbray). Earp is a supmely calm figure, not someone driven by a ameless hatred (as is the case of the Western eroes in the films of Anthony Mann).

Indeed, violence linked to the notion of a ersonal quest hardly exists at all in Ford's lms. Killings, even woundings, are rare. Not a ngle Indian is seen to be killed or wounded in *he Wore a Yellow Ribbon*. In *Two Rode Together* 1961), Sheriff McCabe (James Stewart) fires nly two revolver shots – the only gunshots in he film. Ford could never conceive a scene like he one in Anthony Mann's *The Man From aramie* (1955) where Stewart's hand is aimed. Violence is never a goal in Ford's films r a means of self-fulfilment, but a duty or a ast resort. When violence is inescapable, Ford

bove: in My Darling Clementine *Henry onda portrayed Wyatt Earp as a balanced, ensive peace-loving man. Right: a custodian of ie West retires – John Wayne as Captain rittles in* She Wore a Yellow Ribbon *with arry Carey Jr, Joanne Dru and Victor IcLaglen. Below: Travis (Ben Johnson) and enver (Joanne Dru) in* Wagonmaster

a township whose chief aim is to establish a society of law and order – all those people who, whether consciously or not, have helped to build the United States and whose names and faces have been forgotten. And so it is their work that the films celebrate. This work may not be exalting; it is often thankless, seldom on a big scale, but it is stamped with a day-to-day heroism.

The homing instinct

Most of Ford's pictures are based on and perpetuate a theme that seems to haunt his last Western, *Cheyenne Autumn* (1964) – his elegy on the dispossessed Indians who seek to reclaim their ancestral lands – and that is the need not simply to build or see something through to its conclusion, but to arrive at the possession of a piece of land, a home or hearth, or perhaps simply a rocking-chair, which is exactly what is sought by Mose (Hank Worden) in *The Searchers*. There is also a need to fight against enemies and the elements to keep possessions in order to understand their complete value.

gible proof of the need to affirm publicly the ownership of a place, especially since it could be taken away at any time – as Lars Jorgensen (John Qualen) remarks in *The Searchers*.

The same motivation underlies Ford's fondness for landscapes that are immutable, notably the desert and rocky outcrops of Monument Valley, his favourite location. It is almost as if the film-maker shares with his characters the desire to possess these vast terrains in order to gain a profound appreciation of stability.

Even that antithesis of the Ford hero, Ethan Edwards in *The Searchers*, who can find no place for himself in stable society, is concerned with its continuation. In this fragmented, poignant film – the only one of Ford's based on a notion of individualism – Ethan sets himself against the ordered life and is seemingly involved in a desperate struggle to remain a loner, a rebel. After a hopeless search for his niece that lasts ten years, Ethan finally understands the uselessness of his revolt. He cannot bring himself to kill the girl when he finds her, tainted though she may be by living with an

Indian 'buck' and therefore a threat to white society. Because he is so concerned to preserve the wholeness of the homestead, he does not realize that the people who made it what it was, and thus its very nature, have changed. There is no place for him and after returning Debbie to the community he disappears, leaving the new generation represented by Martin Pawley to take over.

Exiles and nomads

Ethan is just one of scores of exiles that struggle to preserve society in Ford's films. Others include Irish and European immigrants who dream of gaining some sort of new birthright in America. In *The Man Who Shot Liberty Valance* (1962), restaurant-owner Peter Ericson (John Qualen) actually leaps for joy on hearing the news that he has earned his American citizenship. Ford's universe is also peopled by rootless characters who wander aimlessly – like the sailors in *The Long Voyage Home* (1940). Among these exiles there is even a tribe of Indians: the Comanches of *The Searchers* are Indians who have no territory;

they are constantly on the move. There is also the immigrant prizefighter (John Wayne) returning to his home town after killing a man in the ring in *The Quiet Man* (1952), and families put on the road by the effects of the Dust Bowl to look for new work in *The Grapes of Wrath*.

Other characters are exiled in different ways: the crazed white children and women in *The Searchers* who are refused recognition by their kinsfolk as they have been defiled by Indians. There are also the soldiers for whom the bugle song of retreat in *She Wore a Yellow Ribbon* and *The Wings of Eagles* (1957), or disgrace in *Fort Apache*, sounds a little like exile.

In Ford's films it is not only characters that may be uprooted but entire nations and historical periods. The director has often returned to moments when a social class, or indeed a whole race – in *Cheyenne Autumn* the whole Indian community is oppressed and exiled – is on the brink of extinction. Cheyenne autumn, Welsh twilight – these are both situations from which men and women are forced away to find new means of survival. In *How Green Was My Valley* (1941), industrial strife disrupts the working community and the idyllic family life of the Morgans in the Welsh village where they live at the turn of the century. The youngest son, Huw (Roddy McDowall), whose childhood provides the basis of the story, must finally follow his brothers and move on to pastures new.

Ford portrays people trying to remain faithful to themselves, and to their way of thinking, even when threatened by great historical upheavals. In this respect he may be a spiritual relative of the great Soviet director Donskoi.

Above left: an inaptly titled Belgian poster for The Searchers; *the film is less concerned with Debbie and her 'imprisonment' by Indians than with Ethan, who is a 'prisoner' of his obsession with finding her. Right: the killing of Liberty (Lee Marvin) – but not by Stoddard (James Stewart) – in* The Man Who Shot Liberty Valance. *Below: John Wayne and William Holden in* The Horse Soldiers, *one of Ford's poetic tributes to the US Cavalry*

Filmography

As Jack Ford: **1914** Lucille Love – the Girl of Mystery (serial) (prop man; possible credits for act; stunts; ass. dir); Lucile/Lucille, the Waitress (series of four films: She Wins a Prize and Has Her Troubles; Exaggeration Gets Her Into All Kinds of Trouble; She Gets Mixed Up in a Regular 'Kid Kalamity'; Her Near Proposal) (credited as dir. in some sources); The Mysterious Rose (act. only). **'15** The Birth of a Nation (act. only); Three Bad Men and a Girl (act. only); The Hidden City (act. only); The Doorway of Destruction (act; +ass. dir); The Broken Coin (serial) (act; +ass. dir). **'16** The Lumber Yard Gang (act. only); Peg o' the Ring (serial) (act. only); Chicken-Hearted Jim (act. only); The Bandit's Wager (act. only). **'17** The Purple Mask (serial) (ass. dir); The Tornado (+act; +sc); The Trail of Hate (dir. copyrighted to Ford, no screen credit; +act; +sc); The Scrapper (+act; +sc); The Soul Herder (reissued as short 1922); Cheyenne's Pal; Straight Shooting (reissued as short Straight Shootin', 1925); The Secret Man; A Marked Man; Bucking Broadway. **'18** The Phantom Riders; Wild Women; Thieves' Gold; The Scarlet Drop (GB: Hillbilly); Delirium (co-dir); Hellbent (+co-sc); A Woman's Fool; Three Mounted Men. **'19** Roped; A Fight for Love; The Fighting Brothers; Bare Fists; By Indian Post; The Rustlers; Gun Law; The Gun Pusher (reissued as short 1924); Riders of Vengeance; The Last Outlaw; The Outcasts of Poker Flats; The Ace of the Saddle; The Rider of the Law; A Gun Fightin' Gentleman; untitled one-reel promotion film for personal appearance tour by actor Harry Carey. **'20** Marked Men; The Prince of Avenue 'A'; The Girl in No. 29; Hitchin'

Above: Indian women robbed of their homes in Cheyenne Autumn, *based on the real tragedy of the Cheyenne. It was Ford's last Western and the last of nine films he shot wholly or partially in Monument Valley*

whose films were usually set in a period of social change or revolution. Generally the protagonists do adapt and overcome the crises they face in Ford's films, but they are often required to make costly sacrifices. In *The Man Who Shot Liberty Valance*, Tom Doniphon (John Wayne) kills the outlaw Liberty (Lee Marvin) but makes it seem as though Ransom Stoddard (James Stewart) has done so. For this noble act Doniphon sacrifices the personal glory of the deed and the girl he loves to Stoddard, lives a lonely life and dies alone.

Ford's desire to celebrate collective effort in his later films was tainted with the cynicism of advancing years, and there are hints of bitterness. Between the winning simplicity of *Drums Along the Mohawk* (1939) – Ford's tribute to the spirit of pioneer America on the eve of the Revolutionary War – and *She Wore a Yellow Ribbon*, there is a great difference in outlook. In the latter Nathan Brittles reconsiders his existence as a cavalry officer and begins to question it, and also doubts the validity of his current mission to subdue the Indians even though he continues to pursue it.

Monuments to America

Ford's heroes age with his work. The last shot of *The Man Who Shot Liberty Valance* is of the elderly Ransom Stoddard crying: doubt and uncertainty are bound up with sadness. Perhaps by the early Sixties, the time of *Liberty Valance*, *Cheyenne Autumn* and *Donovan's Reef* (1963) – a kind of melancholic, sometimes comic, reflection on the past, set in the mythical paradise of a Pacific island – Ford had become aware of his own uprootedness and of his own peculiar state of being an exile within American cinema. Perhaps he also realized that the nature of his work would ultimately remain as unchangeable as his own Monument Valley, but that everything around him was crumbling and disappearing. But when he ceased making pictures John Ford left behind him several of his own enduring monuments to the building of a country: a few massive rocks left in the middle of a vast desert.

BERTRAND TAVERNIER

Posts; Just Pals. **'21** The Big Punch (+ co-sc); The Freeze Out; The Wallop; Desperate Trails; Action; Sure Fire; Jackie. **'22** Little Miss Smiles; Nero (uncredited add. dir); Silver Wings (prologue dir. only); The Village Blacksmith; The Face on the Barroom Floor (GB: The Love Image). **'23** Three Jumps Ahead (+ sc). *As John Ford:* **'23** Cameo Kirby; North of Hudson Bay; Hoodman Blind. **'24** The Iron Horse; Hearts of Oak. **'25** The Fighting Heart (GB: Once to Every Man); Kentucky Pride; Lightnin'; Thank You. **'26** The Shamrock Handicap; Three Bad Men (+ sc); The Blue Eagle; What Price Glory (uncredited add. dir). **'27** Upstream (GB: Footlight Glamour); Mother Machree (+ sound version 1928). **'28** Four Sons; Hangman's House; Napoleon's Barber; Riley the Cop. **'29** Strong Boy; The Black Watch (GB: King of the Khyber Rifles) (silent scenes only); Salute; Men Without Women. **'30** Born Reckless (silent scenes only); Up the River (silent scenes only; + uncredited sc). **'31** Seas Beneath (silent scenes only); The Brat; Arrowsmith. **'32** Air Mail; Flesh. **'33** Pilgrimage; Doctor Bull. **'34** The Lost Patrol; The World Moves On; Judge Priest. **'35** The Whole Town's Talking (GB: Passport to Fame); The Informer; Steamboat Round the Bend. **'36** The Prisoner of Shark Island; The Last Outlaw; Mary of Scotland; The Plough and the Stars. **'37** Wee Willie Winkie; The Hurricane. **'38** The Adventures of Marco Polo (uncredited add. dir); Four Men and a Prayer; Submarine Patrol. **'39** Stagecoach (+ prod); Young Mr Lincoln; Drums Along the Mohawk. **'40** The Grapes of Wrath; The Long Voyage Home. **'41** Tobacco Road; How Green Was My Valley. **'42** Sex Hygiene (Army training short); The Battle of Midway (doc) (+ co-photo); Torpedo Squadron (private Army film not publicly shown); How to Operate Behind Enemy Lines (Office of Strategic Services training film for restricted showing). **'43** December 7th (co-dir) (feature version for Navy; short for public); We Sail at Midnight (doc) (USA-GB: Ford possibly sup. dir. of American version). **'45** They Were Expendable (+ prod). **'46** My Darling Clementine. **'47** The Fugitive (+ co-prod). **'48** Fort Apache (+ co-prod); Three Godfathers (+ co-prod). **'49** Mighty Joe Young (co-prod. only); She Wore a Yellow Ribbon (+ co-prod). **'50** When Willie Comes Marching Home; Wagonmaster (+ co-prod); Rio Grande (+ co-prod). **'51** The Bullfighter and the Lady (uncredited ed. only); This Is Korea (doc) (+ prod). **'52** The Quiet Man (+ co-prod); What Price Glory? **'53** The Sun Shines Bright (+ co-prod); Mogambo; Hondo (uncredited 2nd unit co-dir. only). **'55** The Long Gray Line; The Red, White and Blue Line (short with footage from The Long Gray Line); Mister Roberts (some scenes only). **'56** The Searchers. **'57** The Wings of Eagles; The Rising of the Moon (Eire); The Growler Story (short). **'58** Gideon's Day (GB) (USA: Gideon of Scotland Yard); The Last Hurrah (+ prod). **'59** Korea (doc) (+ co-prod); The Horse Soldiers. **'60** Sergeant Rutledge. **'61** Two Rode Together. **'62** The Man Who Shot Liberty Valance; How the West Was Won (ep. only). **'63** Donovan's Reef (+ prod); The Directors (short) (appearance as himself only). **'64** Cheyenne Autumn. **'65** Young Cassidy (some scenes only); Seven Women. **'70** Chesty: a Tribute to a Legend (doc) (+ interviewer) (shorter version reissued 1976). **'71** Vietnam! Vietnam! (doc) (exec. prod. only).

Directed by John Ford, 1939
Prod co: Walter Wanger Productions/United Artists. **exec prod:** Walter Wanger. **prod:** John Ford. **sc:** Dudley Nichols, from the story *Stage to Lordsburg* by Ernest Haycox. **photo:** Bert Glennon. **sp eff:** Ray Binger. **ed sup:** Otho Lovering. **sup:** Dorothy Spencer, Walter Reynolds. **art dir:** Alexander Toluboff, Wiard Ihnen. **cost:** Walter Plunkett. **mus:** Richard Hageman, W. Franke Harling, John Leipold, Leo Shuken, Louis Gruenberg, adapted from 17 American folk tunes of the 1880s. **mus arr:** Boris Morros. **2nd unit dir/stunts:** Yakima Canutt. **ass dir:** Wingate Smith. **r/t:** 97 minutes. **Cast:** John Wayne (*The Ringo Kid*), Claire Trevor (*Dallas*), John Carradine (*Hatfield*), Thomas Mitchell (*Dr Josiah Boone*), Andy Devine (*Buck*), Donald Meek (*Samuel Peacock*), Louise Platt (*Lucy Mallory*), Tim Holt (*Lieutenant Blanchard*), George Bancroft (*Sheriff Curly Wilcox*), Berton Churchill (*Henry Gatewood*), Tom Tyler (*Hank Plummer*), Chris Pin Martin (*Chris*), Elvira Rios (*Yakima, his wife*), Francis Ford (*Billy Pickett*), Marga Daighton (*Mrs Pickett*), Kent Odell (*Billy Pickett Jr*), Yakima Canutt (*Chief Big Tree*), Harry Tenbrook (*telegraph operator*), Jack Pennick (*Jerry, barman*), Paul McVey (*express agent*), Cornelius Keefe (*Captain Whitney*), Florence Lake (*Mrs Nancy Whitney*), Louis Mason (*sheriff*), Brenda Fowler (*Mrs Gatewood*), Walter McGrail (*Captain Sickel*), Joseph Rickson (*Luke Plummer*), Vester Pegg (*Ike Plummer*), William Hoffer (*sergeant*), Bryant Washburn (*Captain Simmons*), Nora Cecil (*Dr Boone's housekeeper*), Helen Gibson, Dorothy Annleby (*dancing girls*), Buddy Roosevelt, Bill Cody (*ranchers*), Chief White Horse (*Indian chief*), Duke Lee (*Sheriff of Lordsburg*), Mary Kathleen Walker (*Lucy's baby*).

Apaches have broken out of the reservation and the telegraph wires have been cut. Nevertheless a varied group of passengers boards the stagecoach from Tonto to Lordsburg: Mrs Mallory, a pregnant wife going to join her husband, a cavalry lieutenant; Hatfield, a shady gentleman-gambler; Dallas, a prostitute run out of town by the 'decent' citizens; the bibulous and disreputable Doc Boone, who takes a keen interest in the samples carried by a timid whisky-drummer called Peacock. At the edge of the town they are joined by Gatewood, the pompous local banker. Riding alongside Buck the driver is Curly, a sheriff in pursuit of the Ringo Kid who has broken jail where he has been serving a sentence for a framed murder charge. Just outside town, Ringo himself joins the party (1). The stagecoach heads into Indian country, stopping shortly afterwards at the first staging post (2–3).

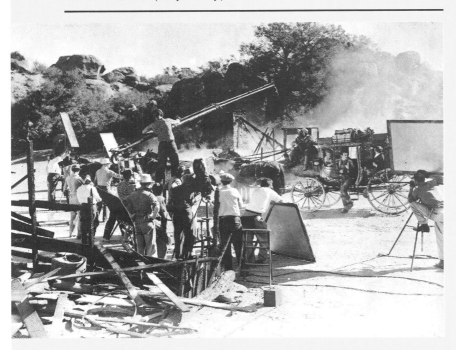

Above: John Ford – standing to the right of the boom-mike operator – filming Stagecoach

Initially, the group is strictly divided between the respectable and the disreputable, but the hazards of the journey temporarily blur the social barriers. Dallas and Doc Boone take charge of the sudden *accouchement* of Mrs Mallory (4). The Ringo Kid falls in love with Dallas, who is touched by his gallantry to her. The whole party is finally united by the Indian attack (5). The cavalry charges to the rescue (6), but not before Hatfield has been killed.

Arriving at Lordsburg, they go their different ways. The Ringo Kid avenges himself on Luke Plummer, the man who had framed him, and is reunited with Dallas. Curly, instead of arresting the Kid, connives with Doc Boone to speed the couple over the border. 'At least they're spared the blessings of civilization,' reflects the philosophic Doc.

Stagecoach has often been credited with reviving the Western in Hollywood in the Forties. Rather, though, it coincided with a whole Western boom, appearing in the same year – 1939 – as *Dodge City*, *The Oklahoma Kid*, *Union Pacific* and *Jesse James*. Even so, when Ford tried to set up the film – his first Western since *Three Bad Men* (1926) – he found the genre was badly out of fashion.

He had bought Ernest Haycox's story, which he found in *Cosmopo-*

1

litan magazine, for $2500. 'It wasn't too well developed,' he recalled, 'but the characters were good.' Producers he approached complained that people no longer went to see Westerns: 'Sure it's a Western, I said, but there are great characters in it. What's the difference whether it's played in the West or wherever?' He took it to RKO where even the powerful Joseph P. Kennedy could not persuade his producers to adopt the project. Walter Wanger, however, who owed a film to United Artists, was finally convinced. Wanger wanted to use Gary Cooper and Marlene Dietrich for the main roles but Ford insisted that it must be cast cheaply, so he hired John Wayne – whose career had so far failed to take off, and who was making five-day Westerns – and Claire Trevor, 'a helluva actress'. Ford surrounded them with fine character players: Thomas Mitchell and Berton Churchill, both stage-trained actors; Donald Meek, George Bancroft, Andy Devine and the cadaverous John Carradine. For every one of them, the role in *Stagecoach* was to prove the most memorable of his career.

Ford himself later drew attention to the faint resemblance of the story to Maupassant's *Boule de Suif*. The critic Welford Beaton was on a better tack, however, when he described the film as '*Grand Hotel* on wheels'. The essence of the story is the interaction of a little group of characters under the stress of a perilous journey.

The structure of the film is very formal. It divides neatly into eight carefully balanced episodes, of which the central and longest is the 24-minute sequence at the Apache Wells staging post with the birth of Mrs Mallory's baby, and the climax is the six and a half minutes of the Indian attack. The expository opening scene, set in Tonto, lasts 12 minutes, during which time every character is carefully and comprehensively introduced.

The characters are also exactly balanced; in one group are the respectable' people – Hatfield, Gatewood (actually an embezzler) and Mrs Mallory; in the other, the 'disreputables' – the Ringo Kid, Doc Boone and Dallas. Buck and Curly, outside the coach, stand aside, a sort of chorus upon the moral debate waged within the coach. The mild little whisky-drummer, too, has a detached function. It is he who states the simple moral of the film: 'Let us have a little Christian charity, one to another.'

The picture was made for $222,000 – $8000 under the assigned budget. The scenes in Monument Valley were completed in four days; the rest was shot on the Goldwyn lot. The Monument Valley days included the extraordinary stunt material staged by Yakima Canutt. Canutt related that after he had performed his most hair-raising feat – jumping onto the stagecoach's lead horse and then, in response to Ringo's rifle shots, falling first to the shafts and then to the ground, allowing six horses and the stage to drive over his prone body – he ran to Ford to ask if the cameras had caught it. 'Even if they didn't,' said Ford, 'I'll not shoot that again.'

At that time there were no specifically equipped camera cars, and ordinary automobiles were used for the amazing scenes where the cameras follow the chase at full speed. The cameramen found to their surprise that in keeping up with the horses they were driving at 40–42 miles per hour.

'I shot it pretty much as it is written,' said Ford, though Dudley Nichols was on the set throughout the film to write – or more likely to cut – dialogue as required. What is striking is the economy of the script. A broken half-line or two will often brilliantly illuminate a character or a situation. At the end, when the characters are returning to their own worlds, Mrs Mallory makes a hopeless attempt to prolong the brief contact with Dallas. 'If there is ever anything …' she begins awkwardly; 'I know,' says Dallas, understanding, but decisively acknowledging the unbridgeable gulf between them in the hypocritical, rigid society of their times.

Stagecoach stands alone for the epic quality both of its panoramas of the West and its human emotions. At the same time it permanently formed Western style. Ford was the first to make use of the spectacular topography of Monument Valley, and was to return to it many times again himself. The final shoot-out, which he had already used in silent films, and was to use again in *My Darling Clementine* (1946), has, since *Stagecoach*, become a cliché.

'It went back to what Wyatt Earp had told me. Wyatt was a friend of mine – in fact I still have his rifle in the corner of my bedroom.'

Ford has always stayed this close to his own West.

DAVID ROBINSON

3

5

6

35

The Codes of the West

The Western is perhaps the USA's greatest contribution to cinema. It has adapted with ease to changes in taste and fashion and continues to provide audiences with thrilling entertainment.

Popular cinema's foremost aim is to entertain its audience. Although a film may contain several different pleasurable elements – songs, witty dialogue, spectacular action, romantic love scenes – its main entertainment value lies in its telling a 'good story'. Often this story follows a common three-part structure: at the beginning the audience is presented with a clear image of stability; this is threatened and disrupted by various forces; by the end, a new order is established. This pattern of events involves, grips and, in its generally happy resolution, releases the audience, allowing it to go home contented. It is largely the presence of

this pleasure-producing sequence which encourages the cinemagoer to tolerate a range of statements about the law, justice, the community, history and sexuality that may be contained in the film. This does not, of course, rule out the possibility that such statements have a deep ideological effect.

The different methods of working through the three main elements of a story are what determine the various genres of popular cinema – comedies, gangster films, horror films, melodramas, and of course Westerns.

The publicity attendant on the showing of a film (for example, reviews, posters and TV programmes about the cinema) helps to prepare the audience in advance; if that film has been billed and written about as a Western, viewers know more or less what to expect before they arrive at the cinema. The star system reinforces this effect; certain names are strongly linked with certain genres. Thus John Wayne and Randolph Scott (virtually throughout their careers), James Stewart and Charles Bronson (at important points in theirs) were closely associated with the Western.

As soon as the audience takes its seat it has specific expectations which begin to be satisfied even before the narrative sequence has been developed. Thus the most characteristic opening (or ending) of a Western is of a rider coming out of (or disappearing into) a part

Top: Charles Bronson, as the half-breed hero of Chato's Land, *adopts the customary pose of the noble savage. Centre: in Gene Autry's films it was easy to tell 'goodies' from 'baddies'. Left: the outlaws find an unusual reception has been prepared for them as they ride into town in* High Plains Drifter

Left: a successful train robbery from Union Pacific. Above left: a gunfighter (Henry Fonda), hired to 'clean up' the town, shoots it out with a couple of cowboys in Warlock. Above: when a well-known 'bad guy' like Lee Marvin (right) sits down to a game of poker, it is not long before more than just money is at stake in Duel at Silver Creek (1952)

oramic landscape. The movement of the rider will invariably be accompanied by a type of music which is different from that which would normally open a gangster movie, a thriller, an epic or a musical. It is a kind of music audiences will immediately comprehend as signifying a Western. The incidental music throughout the film may function as a series of signals easily understood by those members of the audience familiar with other Westerns – for example, the kind of throbbing musical phrase which proclaims that Indians are at hand.

In the early days of the Western the rider's clothes would have conveyed a clear message: good men wore white hats, bad men black. This is less likely nowadays, but as recent a Western as Once Upon a Time in the West (1968) endorsed this code by dressing the main villain entirely in black, though it subverted another – that of casting – by having him played by Henry Fonda, the upstanding Western hero par excellence of such films as My Darling Clementine (1946) and The Ox-Bow Incident (1943).

Although the narratives of all Westerns follow the dominant pattern of order, instability and restoration, they do so in a limited and specific number of ways. In a significant group of Westerns, which includes High Noon (1952), Warlock (1959), Lawman (1971) and High Plains Drifter (1973), the existing order of a town is disturbed by the intrusion of an outside force, such as a gunfighter. Order is restored only by his death or departure; occasionally, as in The Fastest Gun Alive (1956) by him becoming a peaceful member of the community. Another group of Westerns including Winchester '73 (1950), Rancho Notor-

ious (1952), Last Train From Gun Hill (1959) and Chato's Land (1972), are 'pursuit Westerns', with the central pursuing figures very often motivated by revenge for the killing of their kin. Then there are the Westerns concerned with the opening up of the West such as The Covered Wagon (1923), The Iron Horse (1924), Union Pacific (1939), and Western Union (1941). Another key narrative motif has been the journey where a motley group of characters travel together, as in Stagecoach (1939), The Law and Jake Wade (1958) and Ride the High Country (1962); the drama emerges from the internal tensions of the group and the threats to its safety from without.

Clearly these and other key motifs are quite often interwoven. Shane (1953), for example, combines the intrusive gunslinger with another common motif – ruthless cattlemen versus peace-loving farmers.

Within the different types of plot provided by the Western it is possible to identify key narrative set pieces (often points of intense action) common to several of them. These include, for example: the gunfighter's arrival in town and the townsfolk's wary response to him in the saloon; the passing on of gun lore from one generation to another; bank and train robberies; a lynch mob storming the town jail. But perhaps the plot device which has most fired audiences' imaginations is the 'face-off', the climactic gunfight out of which new stability is created. In the Western, as in every other genre, there is a constant tension between repetition and innovation, between immediately identifiable iconography and situations and new variations. Together with the 'order/disruption/new order' narrative form, this tension is the main source of

pleasure for the audience. One of the ways the history of the Western could be written is around the different treatments of the 'face-off': in Stagecoach it happens largely off screen; in Winchester '73 it happens in rocky terrain which causes bullets to ricochet wildly; in Lawman the normal ethical code of the Western hero is abandoned and the 'hero' indiscriminately kills unarmed, wounded and fleeing men. Such differing treatments offer clues to the social mood and attitudes (for example, with regard to screen violence) that prevailed when these films were made.

Conventionally the Western is set in the period between the end of the American Civil War in 1865, and the closing of the frontier in the late 1880s, although certain films made in the Sixties such as Ride the High Country and Lonely Are the Brave (1962) were set in later periods and explored the clash between the old and the modern. This would seem to raise the possibility of looking to the Western as a source of knowledge about American history of this period. However to do so would be simplistic and misleading at any other level than the provision of basic fact – for example, that Wyatt Earp was Marshal of Tombstone and that a gunfight did actually occur at the OK Corral. Like every other popular form, Westerns make statements primarily about contemporary ideological problems; they offer statements about the past for the present. Just as the Western rarely upsets the viewer's narrative expectations, so it rarely subverts the audience's subjective attitude to what it considers 'right' and 'proper', even if these attitudes may be at variance with the realities of life in the USA. For example, it would be difficult to find a Western that resolved its plot-line in favour of the cattleman and at the expense of the homesteader. This is because the most venerated figure in American films, popular literature and political rhetoric is the individual yeoman farmer ploughing his own land. In reality, of course, large corporate interests have significantly more influence on the machinery of government than small farmers. The ideology of agrarian populism is present in other genres – for example a social comedy like Mr Deeds Goes to Town (1936) or a literary adaptation like The Grapes of Wrath

37

(1940), and a melodrama like *All That Heaven Allows* (1955); but by the nature of the thematic terrain traversed by the Western, this ideology is absolutely central – and achieves a religious, almost mystical status in films such as *Wagonmaster* (1950) and *The Westerner* (1940). There is a powerful scene in *The Covered Wagon* in which the wagon train splits, the more sympathetic characters going north to farm land in Oregon, the less sympathetic going south to mine for gold in California. Like

many other Westerns *The Covered Wagon* then had to wrestle with two contradictory sets of ideas, each having great force in American culture. Although homesteading confers nobility, it does not confer wealth. Gold mining confers wealth but not nobility. *The Covered Wagon* cleverly negotiates this contradiction by having its hero strike gold in California and then settle down on a homestead in Oregon, thus reconciling the dominant ideologies of the audience: that of closeness to the land and

Top: the American ideal of the poor but proud settler was celebrated in The Covered Wagon. *Centre left: temperatures reach boiling point within the travelling group of* Ride the High Country. *Above: his parents butchered and his home set ablaze by an outlaw gang, Steve McQueen in* Nevada Smith *(1966) vows vengeance. Left: a cattle-drive from* Red River

material success. This same contradiction negotiated week after week in the TV seri Dallas. Bobbie, the sympathetic member of th Ewing family is often associated with catt and ranching, while the unsympathetic on J.R., is almost exclusively linked with oil an big business. In the absence of homesteading cattle ranching can assume transcendenta significance, underlining the important poir that the various narrative motifs of the Wes ern (or any other genre) have no *absolu* meaning, but only acquire meanings by bein arranged to conflict with each other within th plot structure of particular films.

The Western, one of the first of the popula film genres to emerge, has entertained audier ces for over seventy years. As well as endorsin very traditional American ideologies (such agrarian populism), it has been pressed int service as a form of allegory when dire statements about certain sensitive politic issues were impossible. Thus *High Noon* ha been seen as a comment on the social effects McCarthyism, and *Soldier Blue* (1970) as parable of the Vietnam War. The Western future is assured.   COLIN McARTHU

A man, a horse and a gun

In Hollywood's heyday almost all its leading men were, at some time or another, made to saddle up for a horse opera. Some looked better in the part than others. Those who did it often – like Randolph Scott and Joel McCrea – came to look most at home on the range. It was extremely rare for a star to go against his established image: rather he brought his particular style to the part and the Western was bent into accommodating it. Here is a look at some of the men who contributed to the image of the Western

Robert Taylor

Stand Up and Fight (1939) was a brawling railroad-versus-stage saga which co-starred Taylor as a Maryland aristocrat. This was a change from his usual romantic leads. MGM set about further shedding Taylor's 'pretty boy' image by giving him the title role in *Billy the Kid* (1941), a Technicolor remake of their 1930 production. He looked very uncomfortable in the part and wisely stayed away from the genre until the early Fifties when MGM were making Westerns as a matter of course.

His essential stiffness lent an appropriate sense of dignity to his appearance as a Shoshone Indian victimized by racial prejudice in *Devil's Doorway* (1950). Like a great many stars, Taylor appeared more frequently in Westerns as he grew older and his box-office appeal diminished. Signs of ageing merely gave a suitably weathered look to the characters he played, like the vicious buffalo-hunter in *The Last Hunt* (1956), and the basic appeal of the Western helped overcome his decline in popularity.

Top: Randolph Scott and Joel McCrea stayed in the saddle for many years, eventually playing ageing lawmen in Ride the High Country.
Right: Robert Taylor in an uncharacteristic role as a Shoshone Indian in Devil's Doorway. *Far right: Taylor was more commonly, a gunfighter in his Westerns*

Errol Flynn

The principal Western star on the Warner lot was Errol Flynn who brought the same dashing style and engaging good humour he had displayed in swashbuckling roles to his outdoor pictures. He played the cattle-man turned marshal who helps bring law and order to town in *Dodge City* (1939), a Yankee officer in *Virginia City* (1940) and the reckless, headstrong General in Raoul Walsh's stirring but inevitably whitewashed account of George Armstrong Custer's career – *They Died With Their Boots On* (1942).

Wallace Beery

MGM were never a prolific supplier of Westerns but they produced some to suit the talents of Wallace Beery, who was usually cast as a big-hearted bad guy with a sentimental streak. The formula for his films was to involve him with kids – he reluctantly adopts the son (Darryl Hickman) of a man he has killed in *Jackass Mail* (1942) and he saves a moppet (Margaret O'Brien) from drowning in *Bad Bascomb* (1946). He was frequently given the abrasive character actress Marjorie Main as a foil as in *Wyoming* (1940) in which she turns the rascally outlaw into an honest, teetotalling citizen.

Henry Fonda

Jesse James (1939) co-starred Henry Fonda when he played Jesse's brother Frank – a role he reluctantly repeated in *The Return of Frank James* (1940). Fonda was not interested in such bland, conventional characterizations: he fought with 20th Century-Fox to appear in *The Ox-Bow Incident* (1943) when the studio thought that not only the subject (an indictment of lynch law) but also his subsidiary role as the cowboy observer of the main lynching drama were bound to damage his box-office appeal.

Fonda played a standard Western lead as lawman Wyatt Earp in *My Darling Clementine* (1946) but the routine script was considerably embellished by director John Ford's eye for telling detail. In another Ford film, *Fort Apache* (1948), Fonda yielded the sympathetic part to John Wayne, preferring the more complex role of a wrong-headed cavalry commander (based on General Custer) who leads his men to a brave death.

Fonda then showed his boredom with film work by returning to the Broadway stage; but when he resumed his career he was frequently to be found in Westerns – although he was occasionally cast against type as a bad guy in *Firecreek* (1968) and as a smiling but sadistic villain in *C'Era una Volta il West* (1968, *Once Upon a Time in the West*).

Gregory Peck

In *The Gunfighter* (1950), Gregory Peck's rather solemn and sober manner was put to good effect as he portrayed the ageing gunfighter Jimmy Ringo, hoping to turn over a new leaf and bury the past before it's too late. Peck donned a moustache and alienated his fans; but it was a performance to his lasting credit. Peck was awkward and dull in other Westerns like *Yellow Sky* (1948), where Richard Widmark stole all the attention as a laughing killer, and *Only The Valiant* (1951), where he played a cavalry captain in conflict both with his men and the Apaches.

Top left: Errol Flynn as an Irish adventurer turned marshal in Dodge City. *Top right: Wallace Beery and Darryl Hickman as teacher and pupil in* Jackass Mail. *Above and right: two contrasting roles for Gregory Peck – in a bare-fisted fight in* Only the Valiant *and in a shoot-out in* The Gunfighter. *Left: Henry Fonda, seen here in a publicity shot for* The Tin Star *(1957), always looked at home on the range*

Randolph Scott

An actor of limited range, Randolph Scott found a comfortable niche in the Western. A quiet-spoken native of Virginia, he taught Gary Cooper the right accent to play the title role in *The Virginian* (1929) and was to imbue his own Western characters with flashes of Southern courtesy. After a rambling career that included supporting roles in *Jesse James* and *Western Union* (1941), Scott starred in largely routine Westerns. These films were often about building railroads, like *Canadian Pacific* (1949), or cleaning-up towns, like *Fort Worth* (1951).

In the Fifties, Scott teamed up with the director Budd Boetticher for a series of imaginative Westerns including *Ride Lonesome* (1959) in which he took a back seat to the colourful villains – until the final showdown.

Joel McCrea

With a more substantial career behind him than Scott and taking leading roles, Joel McCrea also concentrated almost exclusively on Westerns in the late Forties. He was less intense than Scott and incapable of suggesting the villainy that Scott had occasionally personified. McCrea had played a handful of Western parts – including *Wells Fargo* (1937), as a trouble-shooter in *Union Pacific* (1939) and in the title role in *Buffalo Bill* (1944) – before deciding that his best bet for the future was to saddle up for good. The Westerns he then made were invariably pleasant but, like the characters he played, rarely forceful and vigorous. *Saddle Tramp* (1950) and *Cattle Drive* (1951) were better than most. He was tempted out of retirement to star with Randolph Scott in Sam Peckinpah's *Ride the High Country* (1962), which is known in Britain as *Guns in the Afternoon* – a haunting valediction in which they played two ageing former lawmen recovering their self-esteem on a final assignment.

Top left: Randolph Scott left behind romantic leads to become a highly convincing cowboy. Top right: William Demarest and Gary Cooper in a comedy Western Along Came Jones. *Above: Gary Cooper went West as a youth – one of his early films was* The Virginian. *Below left: Joel McCrea with Maureen O'Hara in* Buffalo Bill. *Below right: the two most unlikely gunfighters – James Cagney and Humphrey Bogart – in* The Oklahoma Kid

Gary Cooper

The Western suited the taciturn, quiet-spoken style and rangy figure of Gary Cooper. He was born in cowboy country – Montana – and his early film work as an extra, then a supporting player, was mostly in Westerns. He made few of them in his biggest years as a star: Cecil B. DeMille cast him as Wild Bill Hickok in *The Plainsman* (1936) and he chose a comedy Western for his one venture as an independent producer, *Along Came Jones* (1945), in which he played a peaceful cowpoke who is mistaken for a notorious bandit.

Like Fonda, Cooper personified integrity and honesty. He was most memorable in those Westerns where he bided his time before triumphantly asserting himself – finally dealing with Walter Brennan's scene-stealing Judge Roy Bean in *The Westerner* (1940), tired and afraid but ultimately disposing of his enemies in *High Noon* (1952), or as the captive of his evil family whom he finally destroys in *Man of the West* (1958).

Robinson, Cagney and Bogart

Warners' crime stars seemed too much part of a contemporary urban milieu to be cut out for stetsons and six-shooters. Edward G. Robinson did not venture out West until he played a cattle baron on crutches in *The Violent Men* (1955), by which time he had moved from being a gangster to being a character actor; and when James Cagney and Humphrey Bogart were teamed for *The Oklahoma Kid* (1939) it had to be a light-hearted romp. 'Cagney looked like a mushroom under a huge Western hat,' quipped Bogart and the film critic Frank S. Nugent described him in a review as 'not pretending a minute to be anything but New York's Jimmy Cagney, all dressed up for a dude ranch.' Like Robinson, Cagney did not make a serious Western appearance until the Fifties in *Run for Cover* (1955).

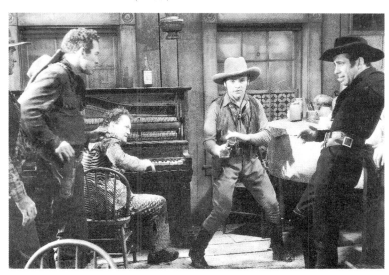

Alan Ladd

The quiet, wistful manner of Alan Ladd adapted admirably to the outdoors, although *Shane* (1953) was to provide him with his only truly memorable Western role as the gunman who sides with the victimized homesteaders. Nevertheless, in *Branded* (1950), he showed real flair for handling the laconic dialogue of the genre. 'You got any friends?' Ladd's saddle tramp is asked. 'My guns', he replies. 'Kinsfolk?' 'My horse.' It was the authentic voice of the Western loner.

John Wayne

The stars of B Westerns generally learned to ride a horse and speak a line comfortably, but their scripts rarely allowed them to make any lasting impression as screen Westerners. Perhaps the most impressive of all Forties Western stars, John Wayne had to escape from the B feature assembly line in order to show what an authoritative figure of the Old West he could suggest. His Ringo Kid of *Stagecoach* (1939) was a straightforward study of a callow, likeable youth. What emphasized his contribution was John Ford's dramatic way of introducing him in a tracking shot as he halts the stage, as well as the climactic gunfight in Lordsburg in which the Ringo Kid acts on his own in shooting it out with the double-crossing Plummer gang.

Even in *Fort Apache* Ford was making fairly elementary use of Wayne's talent as the easygoing Captain Kirby York who clashes with his superior officer (Henry Fonda). It took Howard

Above left: Shane, the story of a mysterious gunfighter, gave Alan Ladd a typical role as a 'loner' hero. Above: Frenchy (Marlene Dietrich) clings to Tom Destry (James Stewart) in the spoof Western Destry Rides Again. Right: Stewart could be the epitome of the tough cowboy, usually portraying the good guy with the mean streak, as in Winchester '73. Below: John Wayne is, perhaps, the actor most identified with Westerns – whether as a youth (left) in The Dark Command *(1940) or as an ageing cattle boss (right) in* Red River

Hawks to show that Wayne could play a complex, intense role. In *Red River* (1948) Wayne's Thomas Dunson was an ageing figure of unyielding stubborness and rock-hard determination; a man who does the 'wrong' things for reasons the audience understands and sympathizes with; a man who is prepared to shoot the adopted son (Montgomery Clift) who has taken his herd away from him.

The lesson was not lost on Ford who gave Wayne another part in which he played a far older man than his actual years – Captain Nathan Brittles, who was coming to the end of an honourably long career – in *She Wore a Yellow Ribbon* (1949). Under Ford's guidance, Wayne spoke, moved and acted like an old man. It was a performance he was not to better, although his portrayals of the embittered Ethan Edwards in *The Searchers* (1956) and the flamboyant Rooster Cogburn in *True Grit* (1969) were as memorable.

ALLEN EYLES

James Stewart

The considerable reputation which James Stewart had for comedy he brought to one Western, *Destry Rides Again* (1939), when he played the gangling tenderfoot who unexpectedly tames a town. He had also developed a rather lazy, amiable image before he turned to Westerns with a vengeance. For such a softspoken, mild-mannered figure to erupt with such fury at the sight of his hated brother in *Winchester '73* (1950) gave Anthony Mann's Western considerable added impact.

Stewart was directed by Mann in other fine Westerns which were mostly filmed on location: *Bend of the River* (1952), as a reformed outlaw; *The Naked Spur* (1953), as a bounty hunter; *The Far Country* (1954) and *The Man From Laramie* (1955). *Broken Arrow* (dir. Delmer Daves, 1950) also contributed to this astonishing and highly successful change of career direction for James Stewart.

"THE DARK COMMAND"

Home on the range

The great Western revival in the Forties reflected America's renewed interest in her history at a time when the war encouraged a spirit of national unity

The successful revival of the Western in 1939 may be ascribed to the mood of the times. War, for the Americans, was on the distant horizon. Europe was dominated by dictators, and alien doctrines were abroad. It was a time when men's minds turned to the nature of 'Americanism' and in particular to the nation's history and its values. It is significant that the Western, celebrating the heroic period of American expansion and highlighting its distinctive qualities of democracy, determination and self-reliance, now eclipsed the distinctly un-American swashbuckler. The latter genre, with its gentlemen heroes adventuring in the aristocratic and hierarchic world of Old Europe (a continent the Americans were currently inclined to mistrust), seemed suddenly anachronistic.

Warner Brothers, the home of swashbuckling films, put Errol Flynn, the erstwhile star of *Captain Blood* (1935) and *The Adventures of Robin Hood* (1938), into a series of expensive, lavish and vigorously staged Westerns in the wake of his success in *Dodge City* (1939). The following year Flynn was seen in *Virginia City* and *Santa Fe Trail* and went on to make other Westerns later in the decade – *They Died With Their Boots On* (1942) and *San Antonio* (1945).

In a hilarious piece of miscasting, Warners even put James Cagney and Humphrey Bogart into a Western romp called *The Oklahoma Kid* (1939). Cecil B. DeMille, the re-creator of the spectacle and grandeur of the Ancient World, had already contributed to the Western genre in the Thirties with *The Plainsman* (1936) and *Union Pacific* (1939). He followed these films with a tribute to the Canadian lawmen in *North West Mounted Police* (1940) and an epic celebration of America's own colonial past in *Unconquered* (1947).

During the war years, all the Hollywood studios contributed to the Western boom. 20th Century-Fox specialized in grand historical epics. They produced *Brigham Young* (1940), dealing with the Mormon trek to Utah in the 1840s, *Western Union* (1941), showing the creation of the telegraph system across the West, and *Buffalo Bill* (1944), a heavily fictionalized account of the career of the frontier scout, buffalo hunter and showman.

The creation by pioneers of the great new western states was celebrated in Columbia's *Arizona* (1940) and *Texas* (1941), MGM's *Wyoming* (1940), Republic's *In Old Oklahoma* (1943) and *Dakota* (1945) and Paramount's *California* (1946). The Texan leader Sam Houston and the frontier scout Kit Carson, two of the most famous heroes of the West, were the subjects of handsome and exciting epics from smaller studios: Republic's *Man of Conquest* (1939) and Monogram's *Kit Carson* (1940).

Other colourful characters of the West flooded onto the screen. Many of them were glamorized outlaws committed to 'truth, justice and the American way' and were pitted against the villains of monopolistic corporations, railroad companies, banks and big business. Among the nineteenth-century bad men canonized on celluloid in the

twentieth century were Billy the Kid in *Billy the Kid* (1941) and *The Outlaw* (1943), Belle Starr in a 1941 film of the same name, the Daltons in *When the Daltons Rode* (1940), the Youngers in *Badmen of Missouri* (1941) and Quantrill's Raiders in *Dark Command* (1940).

The re-establishment of the Western as a cinema staple is demonstrated by the eagerness with which film comedians took the trail West to satirize the conventions of the genre. Among the comic cowboys were the Marx Brothers in *Go West* (1940) and Abbott and Costello in *Ride 'Em Cowboy* (1942). One of the best and most enduring of these films is *The Paleface* (1948), which teamed Bob Hope, in his familiar comic persona of the cowardly, lecherous braggart, and Jane Russell, guying the sultry, sexy, siren image she had created in *The Outlaw*.

During the Forties – and after the war in particular – certain trends began to be discerned, which were to flower in the Fifties when Westerns took on a new sharp edge and intensity. The themes of social significance, sexuality, violence and psychoanalysis testify to a process of maturing on the part of both the industry and the audiences. The move towards more demanding, more complex and more controversial Westerns was to find its full expression in the Fifties.

One of the earliest and most celebrated examples of the socially significant Western, however, was William Wellman's *The Ox-Bow Incident* (1943), a powerful and sombre indictment of lynch law. The obvious artificiality of the studio-shot landscapes emphasized the stark nature of the film's message, and a strong cast, headed by Henry Fonda, vividly portrayed the nature and effects of mob rule.

Equally controversial, but for a different reason, was Howard Hughes' production of *The Outlaw*. The film was designed to launch the career of his newest discovery, Jane Russell, and Hughes devoted much footage to advertising Miss Russell's breasts, which the judge who banned the film in Maryland described as hanging over the picture 'like a thunderstorm spread over a landscape'. After problems with the film censors and the Catholic Legion of Decency, Hughes withdrew the film following its premiere in 1943. He then shrewdly created a full-scale pub-

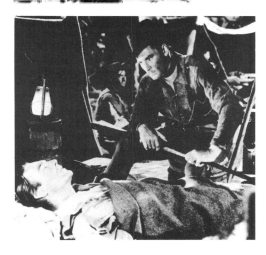

Top: in Texas, two Civil War veterans go into cattle farming. Centre: poster from Fritz Lang's Western Union. *Above: Errol Flynn and Randolph Scott in* Virginia City

Top: in Go West, the Marx Brothers began the film in some semblance of Western costume but soon abandoned it for their more familiar garb. Above: Jack Benny and his manservant, Rochester, in the comedy Western Buck Benny Rides Again (1939). Below: the controversial poster for the first openly sexy Western, The Outlaw

licity campaign to exploit the situation and whip up popular interest in the film. Photographs of Jane Russell in a tight-fitting blouse made her a national sex-symbol long before the film went into release.

The Outlaw finally came out, slightly cut, in 1946 and grossed $3 million in the USA alone. In fact it is a poor film, clumsy, ponderous and slow-moving, the action centring on an all-male triangle, with Pat Garrett pursuing Billy the Kid because he is jealous of Billy's relationship with Doc Holliday. The three men are far more interested in each other and in the prize horse Little Red than in Rio (Jane Russell), the smouldering Mexican girl whose strictly peripheral role is mainly concerned with cooking meals and indulging in a couple of rather suggestive romps with Billy.

Nevertheless *The Outlaw*'s reputation ensured that sex had entered the Western for good. This was confirmed by the success of *Duel in the Sun* (1946), which dealt with the amatory adventures of the half-breed Pearl Chavez (Jennifer Jones), another hot-blooded figure in the tradition of Rio. The film was suffused with a sweaty eroticism and one critic irreverently dubbed it 'Lust in the Dust'.

David O. Selznick sought to repeat the scale and success of *Gone With the Wind* (1939) in *Duel in the Sun* which was directed in the main by King Vidor. Shot in bold Technicolor, this was a Texan *Gotterdämerung* ('Twilight of the Gods'), a veritably Wagnerian Western, full of lurid, blood-red sunsets, breakneck horseback chases, wild dances and intense love-making, punctuated by flashes of lightning and the pealing of bells. The screen constantly

erupted into large-scale action sequences, as wild horses were rounded up, cattlemen confronted the cavalry and a train was derailed. This torrent of activity counterpointed the violent love affair of Pearl Chavez, the spitting, scowling, sneering, tousled, tigerish, half-breed (Jennifer Jones) and Lewt McCanless (Gregory Peck), all-male, all bad, cigarette insolently drooping from the corner of his lips, hat perched jauntily on the back of his head, his whole being oozing an irresistible animal magnetism. Their relationship climaxes in true operatic style with a shoot-out at Squaw's Head Rock, which ends with both mortally wounded, crawling across the sun-baked rocks with bloodied hands to die in each other's arms.

Ritualized violence had always been a key ingredient in Westerns. In the main it was seen as exciting but essentially harmless fun. One of the best examples of this was the prolonged fist fight between hero and villain that was the highlight of the gold-rush Western *The Spoilers* (1942) with John Wayne and Randolph Scott as the protagonists. In the late Forties, however, critics began to voice their concern that violence was becoming much more realistic and brutal. Films like André de Toth's *Ramrod* (1947) were singled out for criticism on this count. The increasingly prevalent use of Technicolor for Westerns further highlighted blood and bruises, although the experience of war had conditioned audiences to accept a greater degree of screen violence.

During the war, public interest in psychology and psychoanalysis had grown and the cinema was quick to capitalize on the phenomenon. The theories of Freud came to the West in Raoul Walsh's

World War II may have conditioned audiences to more violence but the critics protested at the blood and gore in new Technicolor Westerns

moodily impressive *Pursued* (1947) with its hero (Robert Mitchum) dogged by a half-forgotten childhood trauma that is revealed in a complex series of flashbacks. After this, Western heroes could never again be simple, uncomplicated men in white hats riding white horses.

The early Forties saw two classic expositions of the traditional themes of the Western. William Wyler's *The Westerner* (1940) was a slow-moving but beautifully photographed tale that depicted the resistance of decent, hard-working homesteaders to the ruthlessly organized might of the cattlemen. The film offered powerful contrasts between the peaceful, communal celebrations of the settlers (a service of thanksgiving among the cornfields, a cheerful hoedown) and the eruptions of savage violence among the cowboys (trampling down the crops, carousing in the town and beating up their opponents). In the last resort it was a film of character rather than action, exploring the love-hate relationship between Cole Harden, personified by Gary Cooper as the soul of integrity, and Walter Brennan's cunning, hard-drinking old reprobate Judge Roy Bean, dispensing summary justice from a saloon and worshipping the beauty of the actress Lillie Langtry. The relationship ends inevitably but satisfyingly with a final shoot-out on the stage of a theatre where Lillie Langtry is due to appear.

The romance, excitement and glory of war was the subject of Raoul Walsh's sprawling and enthralling US cavalry movie *They Died With Their Boots On*. The film followed the flamboyant career of General Custer from West Point Academy through

JANE RUSSELL MEAN...MOODY...MAGNIFICENT!
in
HOWARD HUGHES' DARING PRODUCTION
THE OUTLAW
ACTION! THRILLS!! SENSATIONS!!! PRIMITIVE LOVE!!!!
JACK BUETEL
THOMAS MITCHELL
WALTER HUSTON

Produced and Directed by HOWARD HUGHES
Screenplay by JULES FURTHMAN

the Civil War to the Western Frontier and his death at the battle of Little Big Horn. In true Hollywood style, this final disaster was turned into an act of heroic self-sacrifice, with Custer knowingly and deliberately sacrificing himself and his troops to protect the main army column from massacre.

Errol Flynn was perfectly cast as the long-haired American general, a swashbuckling paladin of the plains, with a boyish enthusiasm for fighting, a hunger for glory, a delight in gaudy uniforms, a respect for his enemies and a chivalrous devotion to his wife Libby (Olivia de Havilland).

Howard Hawks' *Red River* (1948) provided a prototype hero for the next decade in John Wayne's tough, relentless, revenge-seeking cattle-rancher, Tom Dunson. This is a classic Hawksian film, with its emphasis on professionalism, male cameraderie and dangerous, exciting work on the fringes of civilized society. It re-creates the rigours of the cattle drive – complete with stampede, river crossing and Indian attacks. There are moments of sheer poetry, too, like the start of the drive: mist, dust, dawn, a 180° pan across the waiting herd, and then Dunson yells, 'Take 'em to Missouri, Matt' and Matt's wild yahoo is taken up by each of the drovers in turn in a rapid succession of close-ups as the great herd starts to move.

At the heart of the film is the relationship between Tom Dunson and his adopted son Matthew Garth (Montgomery Clift). When Tom's obsessive desire to get to Missouri leads to rebellion among the drovers, Matt takes over and Dunson pursues him, consumed with bitterness and seeking revenge. The final gunfight between them, however, is frustrated by the quintessential, self-possessed Hawksian heroine (Joanne Dru), who tells them that they really love each other and are not going to kill each other. They accept her logic and are reconciled at the last moment.

John Ford returned from wartime service to begin one of the most richly productive phases of his long career. In *My Darling Clementine* (1946), he took the historical facts of the confrontation between the Earps and the Clantons at the OK Corral and reworked them into a very personal and characteristically complex statement about the bringing of civilization to the West. The Clantons – brutal, lawless and anarchic, ruled with a bullwhip by a tyrannical old patriarch (Walter Brennan) – represent the unacceptable face of the Old West. They are destroyed by the Earps, whose family solidarity and mutual affection is placed at the service of the nascent community. The values of this community are demonstrated in the justly famous sequence in which the decent citizens of Tombstone hold a celebratory square dance in their half-built church, beneath the fluttering flags of the United States. The imagery represents a potent blending of religion, patriotism and community spirit, the cement of the society the Earps are helping to build. Shot, lit and

staged with an austere and strictly ritualized formality, the film undercuts its style with flurries of bustling action and comic interludes like that of the visit of a travelling theatrical troupe.

The same sense of community, allied to a powerful feeling for tradition and the unifying concept of service to the nation, provides the links in Ford's cavalry trilogy: *Fort Apache* (1948), *She Wore a Yellow Ribbon* (1949) and *Rio Grande* (1950). The values of the idealized society which Ford saw embodied in the US cavalry are succinctly encapsulated in the fluttering yellow ribbon, crossed sabres and lusty singing voices of the soldiers, seen and heard behind the credits of *She Wore a Yellow Ribbon*. They are affirmations of its continuity (the ribbon – a symbol of a cavalry sweetheart and hence of the family tradition of service), its role (crossed sabres – an emblem for the maintenance of peace and order), and its community spirit (male voices singing in unison 'The Girl I Left Behind'). It was these values that attracted Ford to the concept of the cavalry at a time when the USA had emerged from World War II to face new problems and rapid social change.

In *The Man Who Shot Liberty Valance* (1962) Ford uses the quotation 'When the legend becomes fact, print the legend'. But in *Fort Apache* Ford is at pains to show the truth behind the legend – in this case, Custer's last stand – at the same time as showing how the legend is born and endorsing the need for heroes and legends in the process of fortifying national memory. Ford lovingly re-creates the rituals of cavalry life – the parades and patrols, regimental balls and dinner parties – and thrillingly stages the battles, charges and Indian attacks as a background to the story of an embittered martinet, Colonel Thursday (Henry Fonda), a thinly disguised Custer figure whose ambition and stubbornness lead the regiment to disaster.

The virtues and strengths of the cavalry are fully embodied by Captain Nathan Brittles (John Wayne) the hero of *She Wore a Yellow Ribbon*. Tough, sentimental, dedicated and professional, he has grown old in the army and given his all to it. The film deals with his last mission – to avert an Indian uprising – before he retires. The mellow autumnal Technicolor in which the film is shot reflects this sense of a career's twilight. If we can see Shakespeare in Prospero breaking his wand and retiring to the country after *The Tempest*, then perhaps it is permissible to see John Ford in the character of Nathan Brittles, the hard-nosed, old professional whose life is his work and whose work is his life. Ford is so devoted to the character of Brittles that he sidesteps the clearly implied tragic ending to recall Brittles from his retirement and have him appointed chief of scouts for the army. *She Wore a Yellow Ribbon* is quintessential Ford and a mature middle-period masterwork that ranks with Hollywood's finest.   JEFFREY RICHARDS

Top left: the new violence of Forties Westerns, as meted out by Joel McCrea to Lloyd Bridges in Ramrod. *Top: the opening up of the West in* Brigham Young. *Above: John Wayne and Montgomery Clift in Howard Hawks'* Red River

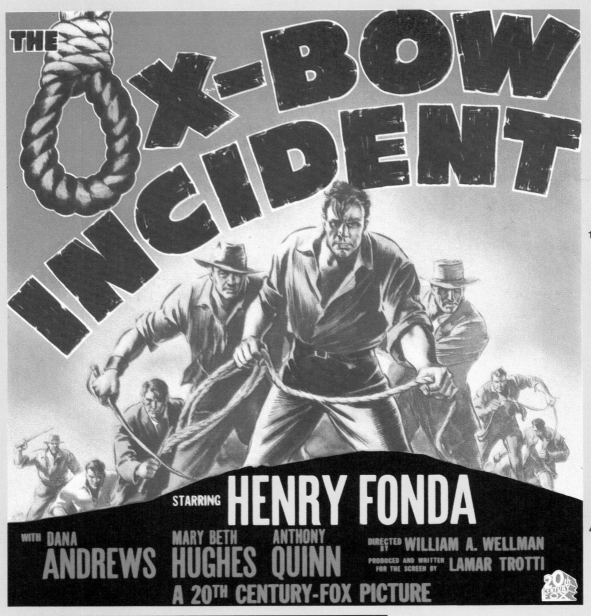

THE Ox-BOW INCIDENT

STARRING HENRY FONDA

WITH DANA ANDREWS · MARY BETH HUGHES · ANTHONY QUINN
DIRECTED BY WILLIAM A. WELLMAN
PRODUCED AND WRITTEN FOR THE SCREEN BY LAMAR TROTTI

A 20TH CENTURY-FOX PICTURE

1

4

Directed by William A. Wellman, 1943
Prod co: 20th Century-Fox. **exec prod:** Darryl F. Zanuck. **prod:** Lamarr Trotti.
sc: Lamarr Trotti, from the novel by Walter Van Tilburg Clark. **photo:** Arthur
Miller. **ed:** Allen McNeil. **art dir:** Richard Day, James Basevi. **mus:** Cyril J.
Mockridge. **r/t:** 77 minutes. Released in GB as *Strange Incident*.
Cast: Henry Fonda (*Gil Carter*), Dana Andrews (*Martin*), Mary Beth Hughes
(*Rose Mapen*), Anthony Quinn (*Mexican*), William Eythe (*Gerald*), Henry
Morgan (*Art Croft*), Jane Darwell (*Ma Grier*), Matt Briggs (*Judge Daniel
Tyler*), Harry Davenport (*Arthur Davies*), Frank Conroy (*Major Tetley*),
Marc Lawrence (*Reverend Farnley*), Francis Ford ('*Dad*'), George Chand-
ler (*stage driver*)

William Wellman's celebrated po-
lemic against lynch law has ar-
bitrarily been described as the first
'psychological' Western. The claim
is as dubious as it is vague, since at
least two earlier examples of the
genre, *White Gold* (dir. William K.
Howard, 1927) and *The Wind* (dir.
Victor Sjöström, 1928), have been
similarly cited.

The Ox-Bow Incident's true significance lies in the fact that it was the
first Western of any importance to
deal uncompromisingly and in a
literate manner with a social issue,
forsaking completely the escapist
trappings, heroism, high idealism
and black-and-white morality of the
traditional Western. It was also the
first to delve deeply into the minds
and motives of a variety of realistic

characters confronted with a situation completely outside their normal experience.

More aptly, some commentators
have called Wellman's film the first
'anti-Western', i.e. a social drama
which exploits the Western formula
to criticize modern social evils. As
such it did indeed presage a new
trend in the Western form, herald-
ing the strain of introspective Westerns of the Forties and Fifties –
which included Raoul Walsh's *Pursued* (1947) and *Colorado Territory*
(1949), Wellman's own *Yellow Sky*
(1948), John Sturges' *The Capture*
(1950) and, most notably, Henry
King's *The Gunfighter* (1950) and
Fred Zinnemann's classic, *High
Noon* (1952).

The Ox-Bow Incident's closest

antecedent was Fritz Lang's con-
demnation of bigotry and mob violence, *Fury* (1936), although Wellman himself had already rehearsed
the lynching theme in his 1932 film,
The Conquerors, in a scene regarded by Western historian William K. Everson as:

'. . . so starkly designed and lit,
and so casually under-played, that
it quite outshines the more carefully
and lengthily constructed lynching
scenes in . . . *The Ox-Bow Incident*.'

Lynching had of course occurred
as a theme in other, earlier Westerns, such as *The Virginian* (dir.
Victor Fleming, 1929), in which the
hero (Gary Cooper) supervises the
hanging of his best friend for steal-
ing cattle. The difference, as ex-
emplified by *Fury* and *The Ox-Bow
Incident*, is that a decade of rapidly
growing social consciousness in
America had turned the act from
one of barely questioned rough justice into something that was abhor-
rent to a civilized society. This is
further emphasized in *The Ox-Bow
Incident* by the fact that, despite the
sympathetic presence of Henry
Fonda, the film has no hero in the
conventional sense. As Robert
Warshow points out in his essay
The Westerner:

'. . . a hero would have to stop the

lynching or be killed in trying to stop
it, and then the ''problem'' of lynching would no longer be central.'

In other words, every participant
in the hanging in *The Ox-Bow Incident* is to blame, whether he or she
approves of the deed or not.

In making the film, Wellman and
his scriptwriter Lamarr Trotti (who
also scripted *Yellow Sky*) remained
as faithful as possible to the original novel by Walter Van Tilburg
Clark. Wellman felt strongly enough
about the project to have purchased
the rights to the book himself. He
spent many months touting it round
the studios before Darryl F. Zanuck
accepted the property for 20th
Century-Fox. Zanuck undoubtedly
recognized that it would fail at the
box-office, being totally out of key
with the escapist fantasies and op-
timistic, patriotic dramas which
were then the almost-exclusive
wartime fare, but perhaps saw its
worth in terms of the prestige the
film would bring to the studio.

The timing of the production had
a crucial effect on the final script.
Despite its general fidelity to
Clark's book, the screenplay ultimately shied away from the novel's
utter pessimism and total condem-
nation of human fallibility. Many
commentators have pointed out
how the film softens and sentimen-
talizes Clark's harsh message (notably in Fonda's reading of the letter
written by the victimized Martin,
which does not occur in the book)
and offers humankind's conscience

The scene is Nevada in 1885. The men of Bridger's Wells are roused to hatred and revenge when they learn that a local rancher, Kincaid, has been murdered by cattle rustlers. With the sheriff out of town, the townsfolk raise a posse (1), despite protests by one of them, Arthur Davies, that their action is illegal. Gil Carter and Art Croft, two riders passing through, reluctantly agree to join the manhunt to prevent suspicion falling on them (2).

The posse comes upon three men – an old half-wit, a Mexican and their leader, Martin (3). Martin claims to have bought cattle from Kincaid to stock a derelict ranch, but has no bill of sale to back up his story.

Although he protests their innocence, the three are condemned to be summarily hanged (4).

Some support is aroused for the accused men, but a sadistic ex-Confederate officer, Major Tetley, makes an eloquent case for the lynching (5). With only seven of the mob voting to await the sheriff's return, the men are hanged from a tree (6, 7).

Too late, the sheriff arrives with word that Kincaid is not dead, only hurt, and that the real culprits have been apprehended. The mob disperses in shame, Tetley commits suicide and, back in the saloon, Gil Carter reads aloud a letter written by Martin to his wife (8). He then rides out with Art to deliver it.

ray of hope where Clark gives one. But in Wellman's defence, it has to be noted that an American audience could hardly have been expected to swallow an implicit indictment of itself as inherently evil at a time when it was battling against evil incarnate in the shape of German and Japanese fascism.

Another criticism levelled at The Ox-Bow Incident is its preponderant use of studio 'exteriors' and the resultant artificiality these give to the film's appearance. But apart from their practicality in allowing Wellman to control his night-scene lighting, it may be equally argued that the studio sets enhance the nightmarish atmosphere of the film and lend to the central scenes an apt expressionistic quality.

Aside from these points, what is important about The Ox-Bow Incident is that, in its modest 77 minutes, it irrevocably altered the nature of the Western, remaining one of the few qualified to support to the full the director Sam Peckinpah's assertion that 'the Western is a universal frame within which it is possible to comment on today'.
CLYDE JEAVONS

The Great Western Myth

Despite sporadic attempts by early Western directors and stars to re-create the Old West as it really was, film audiences demanded romance rather than realism and the genre soon evolved its familiar glamorized style

The gunfighter strides through the swing doors and up to the bar of the Western saloon. 'Leave the bottle,' he snaps as he orders a whisky from the awed bartender. The atmosphere cools perceptibly. And, assuming there is time before someone inevitably takes the opportunity to draw a gun on the gunfighter while he is supposedly off-guard, he casually tosses down a coin in payment.

How much a shot of whisky cost in the Old West depended, obviously, on questions of supply and demand, with prices rocketing in boom towns or on the remoter fringes of the wilderness. But the movie hero never deigns to ask or to wonder uneasily whether he can afford the drink as well as a meal and a hotel room. Unthinkable that John Wayne should have to scratch around in his trouser pocket for the right coins; unimaginable that he should wait, like any common mortal, for his change.

Like so many other gestures in the Western, the coin tossed on to the counter is a ritual designed to suggest not merely insouciance and authority, but an aura of legend. The characters in Hollywood's West may boast a vivid variety of eccentricities and mannerisms but, as with the inhabitants of Lewis Carroll's looking-glass world, their actions are patterned to the formal requirements of a chessboard.

Marauding Indians, for instance, almost invariably show themselves on a distant skyline before whooping down on the trail, obligingly giving the good guys a head start in the chase and the audience an anticipatory thrill of menace. It was John Ford who commented, of the climactic pursuit in *Stagecoach* (1939), that in actuality the Indians would probably simply have shot the stage's horses, in which case there would have been no chase, no last-minute rescue by the cavalry, and no movie.

Enduring as the notion of the gunfight remains in the movies, few real-life gunmen were ever likely to have been so careless of their own survival as to stalk solemnly towards each other from opposite ends of a dusty street, observing the unwritten rule that the other (the bad guy) must make the first move. The code of the West not withstanding, such real-life heroes from history as Wyatt Earp and Billy the Kid were by no means averse to shooting their man in the back.

Way out East

The first Westerns were really 'Easterns' imitating *The Great Train Robbery* (1903), which had been filmed on a somewhat suburban stretch of the Delaware-Lackawanna Railroad in New Jersey. More correctly described as adventure stories concentrating on hairraising action, these films created a tradition not so very far removed from the great serials (like *The Perils of Pauline*) with stars such as Tom Mix playing slick, spotless supermen, equally prepared to deal with cattle rustlers, runaway sports cars and pursuing aeroplanes. Another star, Broncho Billy Anderson, presented a rougher and tougher persona and was not given to the outlandish superstar costumes worn by Mix, but he starred in a series of films that adopted a very similar adventure formula. As early as 1909, however, insisting that Westerns should be shot in the West, Ander-

Right: Tom Mix Westerns like this 1914 two-reeler were full of flashy stunts and showmanship but owed little to the real West. Below: the star who took the Western out West – Broncho Billy Anderson in The Cowboy and the Squaw *(1910)*

son moved his locations to Colorado. Then in 1911 the director Thomas Ince bought the 18,000-acre Santa Monica ranch which he turned into 'Inceville'. Along with the ranch came the Miller Brothers' 101 Ranch Circus, liberally stocked with the authentic cowboys, Indians, covered wagons, horses, buffalo, guns and costumes Ince needed to match the Western landscapes at his disposal in California's Santa Ynez canyon.

Today, watching these little Westerns pro-

duced by Ince, the viewer is struck first an foremost by the almost tangible sense the yield of a world in the making. Rough, tur bledown shacks huddle together in the midd of a bleak and dusty wilderness. Rock canyons backed by towering mountains su gest mysteries as yet unexplored. Grey ar rangy, the strong, silent men who gather these little townships seem hardly to belor there, but to be seeking temporary rest befo pushing on to make new explorations, ne discoveries. It does not take any great stretch the imagination to see here what the ear pioneers saw when they heard how others, little ahead of them, were carving a garden o of the wilderness, and how little clusters of lc cabins were rapidly mushrooming into citie

How the West was lost

This cinematic vision, rich in nostalgia, le directly to the first two epic Westerns, Jam Cruze's *The Covered Wagon* (1923) and Fore *The Iron Horse* (1924). Both films made valia efforts to ensure authenticity in setting ar detail as they turned the pages of history whie recounted the inspiring story of how courag patience and endurance ensured that the We was finally won. But, of course, the spread civilization across America was also a story widespread individual frustration. Driven fii by land hunger, then by gold fever, pionee swept westwards only to find that the con me land-grabbers and politicians had got the first, picking up the fortunes and leavir scattered crumbs.

Given the confused circumstances in whie land-grabbing companies appeared ever where to develop territories claimed by tl original thirteen States but theoretically b

Inset above: the dentist and gunfighter John 'Doc' Holliday: he was played by Stacy Keach (above) in Doc (1971) and Kirk Douglas (top, far right) in Gunfight at the OK Corral (1957). Bottom right: rustler and lawman Wyatt Earp: he has been portrayed by Henry Fonda (above, far right) in My Darling Clementine and James Stewart (far right) in Cheyenne Autumn (1964). Below: Billy the Kid, represented as a mindless psychopath by Michael J. Pollard (below right) in Dirty Little Billy (1972) but less accurately by Roy Rogers (right) in Billy the Kid Returns (1938)

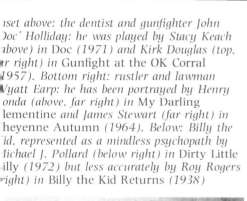

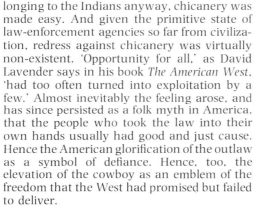

longing to the Indians anyway, chicanery was made easy. And given the primitive state of law-enforcement agencies so far from civilization, redress against chicanery was virtually non-existent. 'Opportunity for all,' as David Lavender says in his book *The American West*, 'had too often turned into exploitation by a few.' Almost inevitably the feeling arose, and has since persisted as a folk myth in America, that the people who took the law into their own hands usually had good and just cause. Hence the American glorification of the outlaw as a symbol of defiance. Hence, too, the elevation of the cowboy as an emblem of the freedom that the West had promised but failed to deliver.

Hart of the West

William S. Hart, who was hired by Ince in 1914, might justifiably be described as the first authentic cowboy star. Unlike Mix, he dressed soberly in drab and dusty chaps with plaid shirt, and although he played a two-fisted hero, his dour, wirily frail, middle-aged presence discounted any flashy superman image. Unlike Anderson, an actor with leanings to the theatre who could barely ride, Hart had lived and worked as a cowboy in Kansas. He immediately demanded, and achieved, a greater authenticity in setting, costume and even story than anyone had previously thought necessary.

Hart's screen persona, however, remained as unvaryingly inauthentic as those of Anderson and Mix. He might be playing a ruthless outlaw, but the plot ensured that he would be

Above left: the famed Indian fighter George Custer, portrayed as a dashing hero by Errol Flynn (top left) in They Died With Their Boots On *and as a conceited blunderer by Richard Mulligan (above) in* Little Big Man *(1970), starring Dustin Hoffman*

accepted as the unmistakable hero of the piece by having his misdeeds occur before the action began; on screen Hart's characters were almost invariably irreproachable. As films and audiences increased in sophistication, such precautions became unnecessary. Like the gangster, who for the average American incarnated his impatience with the Prohibition or his rebellion against the frustrations of the Depression, the outlaw once more came to represent the spirit of independence. And on screen he was free to rob, cheat and kill, and still remain the hero.

To achieve this desirable end, some tailoring of the facts was necessary. In reality, the cowboys – 'slaves to a particularly stupid and unattractive animal', as David Lavender described the cattle-herders – hardly sprang to mind as the image of liberty; so they were generally portrayed as footloose and fancy free, roaming not only the range but the entire West as the spirit moved them. In reality, the gunfighter – whether hired assassin or lawman, with the latter usually drawn from the ranks of the former – was hardly an inspiring object for admiration; so he was given the code of the West, ensuring that he maintained a sense of fair play worthy of the English public-school system. The real women

of the West – for the most part penny-pinchir wives or money-grubbing whores – can rare have matched the glamour, virtuous inno cence and spirited emancipation of th heroines invented as worthy counterparts romance to all the dashing screen Billy th Kids, Wyatt Earps and George Custers.

For a few years, as such legendary survivo of the Old West as Buffalo Bill Cody ar Emmett Dalton (last of the notorious Dalt gang) became involved with the early cinem an authentic record of the West seemed

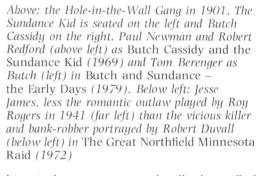

Above: the Hole-in-the-Wall Gang in 1901. The Sundance Kid is seated on the left and Butch Cassidy on the right. Paul Newman and Robert Redford (above left) as Butch Cassidy and the Sundance Kid (1969) and Tom Berenger as Butch (left) in Butch and Sundance – the Early Days (1979). Below left: Jesse James, less the romantic outlaw played by Roy Rogers in 1941 (far left) than the vicious killer and bank-robber portrayed by Robert Duvall (below left) in The Great Northfield Minnesota Raid (1972)

historical personages were hardly the stuff of which heroes were made, to query the feasibility of certain standard trade marks of the gunslinger's cinematic art, to try to assess the rights of the bitter conflict between white man and red. But such films are rare among the classics of the Western.

Mythical heroes

So Custer was a blind, vainglorious fool who led his men like lambs to the slaughter at the Little Big Horn; who cares when, in the swashbuckling person of Errol Flynn with sabres rustling and all pennants flying, he heads the gloriously doomed charge of the Seventh Cavalry in Raoul Walsh's *They Died With Their Boots On* (1942)? So Doc Holliday was really a dentist, a sadist and a peculiarly ruthless killer; who cares when one can have the imaginative alternative of Victor Mature's tubercular doctor in John Ford's *My Darling Clementine* (1946), clad in Luciferian black, coughing delicately into his spotless handkerchief, and redeeming his sins by performing an operation on a bar-room table before joining the forces of good in the gunfight at the OK Corral?

It is no accident that John Ford should have earned an unassailable reputation as the maker of the greatest Westerns of all. More concerned with nostalgic memory than with historical truth, Ford invariably obeys the dictum of the newspaper editor in his own *The Man Who Shot Liberty Valance* (1962): 'When the legend becomes fact, print the legend.' Ford does not create the West as it was, but the West as it should have been. And that is what the Western genre is all about. TOM MILNE

stinct possibility. The reformed bank robber l Jennings, for instance, starred in a number films between 1908 and 1919 that reflected s disenchanted view that: 'There wasn't any amour in the life; there was much that was d, much that was indifferent, and some that as good. But there wasn't any romance out it. It was hard, sordid and tragic'.

Stills of Jennings present him as anything it a heroic figure – a sour, runtish desperado ho clearly incarnates his own view that ime did not pay, even in the West, and that a

bank robber was no dashing hero. One of his films, *The Lady of the Dugout* (1918), implies a desperate, degrading poverty in the promised land that no other Western has ever matched: the lady in question, abandoned by her husband, lives with her child in a hole dug out of the soil of the prairie. But audiences wanted romance. Al Jennings faded from view and the West of mythology usurped the throne.

Since then, carpers have constantly sniped at the liberties taken with truth. Some films have been made to demonstrate that certain

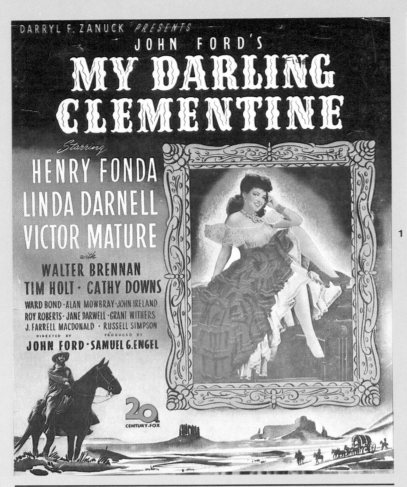

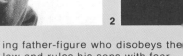

Directed by John Ford, 1946

Prod co: 20th Century-Fox. **prod:** Samuel G. Engel. **sc:** Samuel G. Engel, Winston Miller, from a story by Sam Hellman based on the book *Wyatt Earp, Frontier Marshal* by Stuart N. Lake. **photo:** Joseph P. MacDonald. **ed:** Dorothy Spencer. **art dir:** James Basevi, Lyle Wheeler, Thomas Little, Fred J. Rode. **cost:** Rene Hubert. **mus:** Cyril J. Mockridge. **ass dir:** William Eckhardt. **r/t:** 97 minutes.

Cast: Henry Fonda (*Wyatt Earp*), Linda Darnell (*Chihuahua*), Victor Mature (*Doc Holliday*), Walter Brennan (*Old Man Clanton*), Tim Holt (*Virgil Earp*), Ward Bond (*Morgan Earp*), Cathy Downs (*Clementine Carter*), Alan Mowbray (*Granville Thorndyke*), John Ireland (*Billy Clanton*), Grant Withers (*Ike Clanton*), Roy Roberts (*mayor*), Jane Darwell (*Kate Nelson*), Russell Simpson (*John Simpson*), Francis Ford (*Dad*), J. Farrell MacDonald (*Mac*), Don Garner (*James Earp*), Ben Hall (*barber*), Mickey Simpson (*Sam Clanton*), Fred Libby (*Phin Clanton*), Charles Stevens (*Indian*), Arthur Walsh (*hotel clerk*), Jack Pennick (*stage driver*), Louis Mercier (*François*), Harry Woods (*Luke*).

The gunfight at the OK Corral, Tombstone, Arizona on October 26, 1881, was without doubt one of the most famous events in the history of the American West. It is hardly surprising that John Ford – of all great American film directors the one to show consistently a passion for his country's history – should include it in one of his finest Westerns, *My Darling Clementine*.

Right up to the last moments of the film, when the shoot-out takes place, it is impossible to foresee what is going to happen because the director has managed to portray the central character Wyatt Earp not as the legendary figure that the real gunfight made him, but as an ordinary human being going about his day-to-day activities. In *My Darling Clementine* Wyatt the man is constantly given precedence over Wyatt the hero. The film has none of the usual elements of the Wyatt Earp 'myths' or any vindication of the

triumph of law over the anarchy and violence of the Old West. However, this frees the spectator to draw conclusions that are never explicitly stated and which gain in strength from this apparent indifference. As events unfold on the screen, moral certitude becomes so absolute that Ford is even able to use an audacious ellipsis in the culminating moment of the gunfight: the death of Old Man Clanton takes place off screen, as though the director were only concerned with the eradication of evil in order to be able to release his central character for other adventures.

Whatever the circumstances, Wyatt behaves with dignity and restraint. He is a man who loves peace and tranquility and only accepts a more dynamic role when driven by the brutal killing of his younger brother and the theft of his livestock. In contrast there is Doc Holliday, one of Ford's least

characteristic anti-heroes. Always dressed in black, he is a dandy fascinated by risk, whose search for the absolute has unaccountably led him to a slow and systematic destruction of his talents. He has given up being a doctor and left his fiancée Clementine in order to take refuge in Tombstone. Haunted by the thought of a death that he knows to be close at hand, but still more terrified of braving life, he repeatedly tries to provoke a confrontation that would be fatal to him. Suicidal, identifying himself with Hamlet's agony, uprooted and out of place in this primitive West to which he introduces an element of absurdity and nihilism, Doc Holliday is the complete opposite to Wyatt Earp. In the eyes of civilization he is the man without motive, the poet and the vagabond.

Ford was indisputably one of the cinema's most skilful portrayers of American family life, which he regarded as the institution central to collective living and a reservoir of stable values. It is significant that *My Darling Clementine* begins as a family drama – with the killing of James Earp turning Wyatt and his brothers against the Clanton family. These two clans are also led into conflict by their different ways of life. The Earps are a united family that extends its community-mindedness to their cleaning up of Tombstone and whose profound sense of interdependence even transcends death. On the other hand there are the Clantons, symbolically isolated in the heart of the wild country, pillaging and leading a life as primitive as it is violent. They are dominated by a threaten-

Below: Henry Fonda, John Ford and Cathy Downs on the set of My Darling Clementine

ing father-figure who disobeys the law and rules his sons with fear.

While the Clantons are only united in a violence that alienates them from the community, the Earps merge more and more into the large 'family' of Tombstone, joining in the ceremonies – the church service and the dance – that mark the bringing of peace to the township.

These rituals also bring together a man and a woman, Wyatt and Clementine, and allow them to express their unspoken feelings for each other. Their timid and repressed love is the counterpart of the more tragic love of Doc for Clementine and the sincere but fated love of Chihuahua for Doc. Throughout the film each character pursues another who denies him and continues along the path that he (or she) has carved out for himself. Doc fulfils his destiny and Chihuahua pays for her lie about the medallion, both by dying; Clementine – who comes from the East bringing civilization – stays on in Tombstone as a teacher; and Wyatt finally finds his vocation as a cowboy and decides to take to the trail again.

The last scene of the film could well be Ford's trade mark: a woman stands watching a man disappearing along a road, his lust for adventure not yet satisfied. For Wyatt, the episode in Tombstone was only a stage in his migration, an interval in which he tasted the 'charms' of a civilization for which he does not feel the need for any permanent attachment; at the end he rejoins the majestic scenery of Monument Valley where the first events of the story took place. It is a scenery forever inhabited by the vast family of Ford's heroes and Wyatt goes back to them with regular, peaceful footsteps.
OLIVIER EYQUEM

3

4

6

Driving their cattle west, Wyatt Earp (1) and his brothers make camp outside Tombstone. While Wyatt, Morgan and Virgil are in town, James is shot dead and the herd stolen. Wyatt agrees to become marshal and confronts the Clantons with the murder of his brother (2).

After dumping saloon-girl Chihuahua in a horse trough for spying on his poker hand (3), Wyatt is challenged by her man, gunslinger Doc Holliday (4). But instead of fighting, the two become friends. Pretty Clementine Carter, who was Doc's nurse in his old practice, arrives in town (5) to persuade him to go back East with her, but he refuses and gets drunk. Wyatt takes Clementine to Tombstone's first ever church service and to a celebratory dance (6).

Doc leaves town on his own. Chihuahua blames Clementine and they fight. When Wyatt separates them, he sees that Chihuahua is wearing a medallion (7) taken from James when he was killed. She tells him Doc gave it to her and Wyatt rides after him, wounds him (8) and brings him back. Billy Clanton shoots down Chihuahua (9) when she confesses that it was he who gave her the medallion. Wyatt's shot hits him but he escapes and is pursued by Virgil. Doc prepares to operate on Chihuahua (10). Billy dies and Old Man Clanton kills Virgil. Wyatt finds his body on the street.

Wyatt and Morgan go to the OK Corral for a final showdown with the Clantons (11). Chihuahua has died and Doc joins the Earps. In the shoot-out the Clantons and Doc (12) are killed. Wyatt and Morgan leave Tombstone. Clementine (13), staying on as the new schoolmarm, says goodbye to Wyatt as he rides away.

8

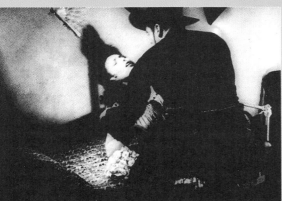

10

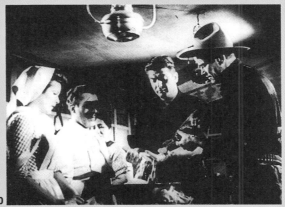

12

13

Mann of the West

His first movies were black thrillers – his last were magnificent epics. But Anthony Mann will surely be remembered, and justly so, for his tragic vision of the West

Although Anthony Mann (1906–67) is regarded primarily as a director of Westerns, notably *Man of the West* (1958) and his films with James Stewart such as *Winchester '73* (1950) and *The Man From Laramie* (1955), he did not direct his first Western until *Devil's Doorway* in 1950. This was eight years after his debut in 1942 with *Dr Broadway*, before which he had worked mainly in theatre.

During the early Forties Mann's work ran the gamut from thrillers to musical comedies, but with *Desperate* (1947) Mann produced the first of an increasingly assured series of *films noirs*, the best of which – *T-Men* (1947) and *Raw Deal* (1948) – are peaks of the genre. Here

Mann perfected a darkly dramatic and expressive visual style whose traces can be glimpsed even in his apprentice works – studio-imposed B-feature material over which he had little control, and where the only possibilities for experiment lay in visual style. It was here that Mann learned how to use the dimensions of *mise-en-scène* to maximum dramatic effect. One example is *The Great Flamarion* (1945) with its ritualistically presented murders and extensive tracking shots which seem to establish more complex relationships between the characters than those indicated by the script; another is *Strange Impersonation* (1946) whose violent underworld milieu prefigures Mann's later.

more accomplished *films noirs*.

But it was with *Desperate* that Mann edge significantly closer to the creation of tha strikingly *noir* ambience that characterizes *Men* and *Raw Deal*. The film contains suc bravura moments as a fight under a wild swinging light bulb, plunging the decor alte nately into darkness and blinding light, a nai biting climax replete with enormous sweat close-ups, and a horribly sinister performanc from Raymond Burr as the lead heavy. With *Men* Mann really came into his own. The stor of two treasury agents infiltrating a counte feiting gang, it was photographed by Joh Alton who also shot *Raw Deal*, *Reign of Terr* and *Border Incident* (both 1949) and *Devil Doorway*. His highly expressive, almost ab stract style of 'painting with light', in whic shadow plays almost as great a role as ligh was pre-eminently suited to Mann's concep

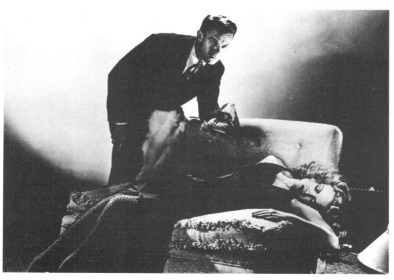

on of a *mise-en-scène* where lighting, com-position, camera angles, editing, everything is rought into maximum dramatic effect, creat-g a powerful sense of imminent danger, mmering violence and underlying tension.

And yet this is not simply a matter of onjuring 'atmosphere': Mann's *mise-en-scène* the perfect visual expression of the universe darkness and evil that these stories inhabit, their inherent pessimism and nihilism hich could never have been expressed by the ript alone in a Hollywood bound by the Hays ode. As it is, *T-Men* is couched in a spurious d moralistic 'documentary' framework, but ann transcends this by visual means, trans-rming what could have been a crudely ropagandist pseudo-realist tract into a ackly imaginative vision of urban night-are, an evocation of a world distinctly off-

balance. The film also contains two seminal Mann scenes in which one of the agents, in order not to blow his cover, has first to deny knowing his wife, and then watch his fellow agent murdered. This is an early glimpse of the tragic paradox at the heart of Mann's heroes which was to appear in all its fullness in the Stewart Westerns – namely, that in order to do what they believe to be right, his heroes risk becoming the embodiment of all they hate.

Raw Deal, too, prefigures the later Westerns in that it is a classic story of revenge. Quite bereft of *T-Men*'s documentary trappings, it is unremittingly bleak and baroque, with a nar-rative recounted by Claire Trevor that beats even Mitchum's in *Out of the Past* (1947, dir. Jacques Tourneur) for resigned fatalism.

The year 1950 marked Mann's transition from *film noir* to Western with *The Furies* (1950) and *Devil's Doorway* followed by *Win-chester '73* – the first of the Stewart cycle comprising *Bend of the River* (1952), *The Naked Spur* (1953), *The Far Country* (1954) and *The Man From Laramie*. These, along with *Man of the West*, starring Gary Cooper, are among the masterworks of the genre. After a relatively undistinguished period throughout the For-ties, the Western was again coming into its

own as major A-feature material, and Mann's early Westerns, with their violent and intense conflicts, their powerful and dramatic sense of landscape and uncompromising vision of the West, are typical of the Fifties Westerns' re-newed vigour.

With *Border Incident* Mann had already shown himself fully capable of handling land-scape as dramatically as cityscape, exploring a far darker side of the West than that shown by Ford. Befitting Mann's essentially dark and tragic vision, his first Western – *Devil's Door-way* – is a sombre epitaph to the Indian, a much bleaker and more uncompromising film than Delmer Daves' better-known pro-Indian *Broken Arrow* (1950), demonstrating with mer-ciless logic that the purpose of law is repression

Left: James Stewart as the fateful Will Lockhart in The Man From Laramie – *one of Mann's intense family sagas with Lockhart the brutalized victim of his own revenge quest. Below left: Mann's medieval epic* El Cid *is the moving story of the 11th-century Spanish knight (Charlton Heston), who here takes as his bride Chimène (Sophia Loren)*

and exploitation, and that political power does indeed flow from the barrel of a gun.

In *The Furies* Mann embarked on the first of his Westerns of intense family conflict. Beneath the story of Barbara Stanwyck's struggle to prove herself the worthy daughter of her tough rancher father, there clearly lies the playing out of a considerable Electra complex, and the film irresistibly recalls that most famous psychological 'Western *noir*' *Pursued* (1947, dir. Raoul Walsh). Both are based on stories by Niven Busch and explore areas usually ignored by the traditional Western. *The Furies* (as its title implies) occupies the merciless world of Greek tragedy. As in Mann's other Westerns, family conflicts are played out on a level that recalls Shakespearian drama, and it is hardly surprising that one of his unrealized projects was a Western version of *King Lear* with John Wayne.

Winchester '73 – like the other Stewart films – is essentially an elemental revenge drama played out against an epic Western landscape which functions as a protagonist in the action, providing a visual correlation of the characters. In these films it becomes possible to speak of the Anthony Mann hero, a solitary, almost schizophrenic figure, propelled at once by violent inner forces and a desire for rest and peace. This is epitomized by *The Naked Spur*, in which Howard Kemp becomes a bounty hunter largely in order to exact revenge upon *himself* for being too human and vulnerable in the past. Often – and especially in *Bend of the River* – the charming villain functions as a reflection of the hero, as his more or less unbalanced alter ego. This is what gives their confrontations such epic power.

To talk of hero or villain may sound simplistic, but Mann operates precisely on a symbolic even mythical level, and this was to stand him in good stead when, with the decline of the Western, he turned to the epic, making *El Cid* (1961) and *The Fall of the Roman Empire* (1964). Indeed, the former is one of the most sheerly beautiful films ever made. Mann's settings constantly stress the archetypal extensions of his dramas, to ritualistic and mythical effect.

Like all legends, Mann's Westerns revolve around the family – in *Winchester '73* Lin McAdam remorselessly pursues his brother who has murdered their father. In *The Man From Laramie* the full Oedipal drama is played out around the Waggoman family, and in *Man of the West* a reformed outlaw kills his adopted father and grotesque 'family' so that he may lead a new life. Central to all these works is the theme of usurpation, of the death of the father. Beneath these conflicts of dynasty with their overtones of classical tragedy, beneath the cycles of death and rebirth of the hero, lie those drives so prominent in Freud's work. But, that apart, Mann's *films noirs*, Westerns and epics are feasts of visual pleasure – spectacular in the true sense of the word, and, as Jean-Luc Godard said of *Man of the West*, 'an admirable lesson in cinema – in modern cinema.'

JULIAN PETLEY

Filmography

1941 Sullivan's Travels (ass. dir.). '42 Dr Broadway; Moonlight in Havana. '43 Nobody's Darling. '44 My Best Gal; Strangers in the Night. '45 The Great Flamarion; Two O'Clock Courage; Sing Your Way Home. '46 Strange Impersonation; The Bamboo Blonde. '47 Desperate (+cosc); Railroaded; T-Men. '48 Raw Deal; He Walked by Night (add. dir. uncredited). '49 Reign of Terror; Follow Me Quietly (co-sc. only); Border Incident; Side Street. '50 Devil's Doorway; The Furies; Winchester '73. '51 The Tall Target; Quo Vadis (add. dir. uncredited). '52 Bend of the River (GB: Where the River Bends). '53 The Naked Spur; Thunder Bay; The Glenn Miller Story. '54 The Far Country. '55 Strategic Air Command; The Man From Laramie; The Last Frontier. '56 Serenade. '57 Men in War; The Tin Star; Night Passage (add. dir. uncredited). '58 God's Little Acre (+co-prod); Man of the West. '60 Spartacus (add. dir. uncredited); Cimarron. '61 El Cid (US-IT). '64 The Fall of the Roman Empire. '65 The Heroes of Telemark (GB). '68 A Dandy in Aspic (GB) (some scenes only; +prod).

High noon in the West

The Western took on a new lease of life in the Fifties, using many varieties of colour film and a wider range of themes, including the good Indian

The early history of the Western is largely associated with B pictures and programmers, aside from the relatively small number of prestige productions like *The Covered Wagon* (1923), John Ford's *The Iron Horse* (1924) and *Cimarron* (1931). An upgrading of the genre during 1939–41 proved short-lived as the war film took over, while many leading male stars were lost to the armed services. But a genuine revival began to develop during the immediate post-war period with prestige productions from David O. Selznick (*Duel in the Sun*, 1946) and Howard Hawks (*Red River*, 1948), and a notable series of Westerns directed by John Ford including *My Darling Clementine* (1946) and *She Wore a Yellow Ribbon* (1949). And by the early Fifties the Western was flourishing as it never had before.

High-quality Westerns, mainly in Technicolor, were produced by all the major studios alongside the last of the cheapie programmers in black and white (soon to be killed off by television), while Westerns from the small independent companies like Republic, Monogram and United Artists often exploited the new, cheap, two-colour processes like Cinecolor and Trucolor. There were still 'serious' pictures in black and white like *The Gunfighter* (1950) and *High Noon* (1952). A new respect for the Indian was a feature of 20th Century-Fox's *Broken Arrow* (1950) and MGM's *Across the Wide Missouri* (1951). The more traditional action film also continued to flourish, as represented by the Audie Murphy cycle of Westerns from Universal. The contribution of veteran directors like Ford and Hawks was matched by experienced men like Anthony Mann, Delmer Daves and John Sturges, who had begun their careers during the Forties, along with a group of younger directors coming to maturity, including Robert Aldrich, Budd Boetticher and Nicholas Ray.

Perhaps more than any other genre, the Western during the early and mid-Fifties reflected that this was a period of transition. The political uncertainties of the post-war years – the Cold War, the Korean War and the election of Eisenhower in 1952, the first Republican President for 20 years – contributed to a new American preoccupation with the national past and a reaffirmation of traditional virtues and values, suggesting a need for old-fashioned escapist Westerns newly bedecked in colour, CinemaScope and 3-D. Yet the film audience was more sophisticated than before and demanded a greater complexity and maturity in Western themes and characterization.

The decline of the old studio system coincided with a greater emphasis on location filming of major features in colour making use of authentic settings; the B feature was virtually abandoned. And many leading directors chose a Western for their first venture into colour, including Delmer Daves' *Broken Arrow*, Anthony Mann's *Bend of the River* (1952) followed by *The Naked Spur* (1953) – both starring James Stewart; Don Siegel's *Duel at Silver Creek* (1952, starring Audie Murphy) and George Stevens' *Shane* (1953). Sets and costumes

were generally less expensive than for other types of period picture, while the colourful landscapes and settings were conveniently close to Hollywood.

As for the cheaper colour processes like Trucolor and Cinecolor, outdoor subjects like Westerns were almost a necessity, for their limitations were more apparent when filming interiors with artificial lighting – not surprisingly, the best ever film in Republic's Trucolor process was Nicholas Ray's Western *Johnny Guitar* (1954), starring Joan Crawford. A Western was often used for the 'trial run' in introducing various new colour processes and other technical innovations. For example, MGM's first production in Ansco colour was *The Wild North* (1951), followed by John Sturges' first colour film, *Escape From Fort Bravo* (1953), also shot in a 3-D version.

Similarly, the first films in the new Warnercolor (a version of Eastman Colour) in 1952 were mainly Westerns. And Pathecolor, yet another version of Eastman Colour, was introduced in 1953–4. The first group of 3-D pictures in 1953 included Westerns such as Raoul Walsh's *Gun Fury* and John Farrow's *Hondo* starring John Wayne. The musical Western *Oklahoma!* (1955) was the first production in the new Todd-AO (65 mm) process as well as the first venture into colour by Fred Zinnemann, who had directed the best-known black-and-white Western of the Fifties, *High Noon*. James Stewart starred in the first Technirama production, *Night Passage*, in 1957; and Westerns also proved ideally suited for filming in the other new processes like Cinema-Scope and VistaVision.

Many of the top male stars who were first discovered and developed by the major studios during the peak years of the Thirties and early Forties had reached an age and maturity by the Fifties which could best be exploited within the Western format. Established Western stars such as John Wayne, Gary Cooper and Randolph Scott appeared in many of their best roles. James Stewart suddenly emerged as a major Western star, after

Top: Jay C. Flippen, Claire Trevor and Kirk Douglas in King Vidor's Man Without a Star *(1955). Douglas gives an aggressive performance as a rugged saddletramp reluctant to recognize that the Old West is dying and that barbed-wire has come to the range to stay forever. Above: in* The Tin Star, *a veteran former lawman (Henry Fonda) tutors an inexperienced sheriff (Anthony Perkins) until he is ready to face the bad guy*

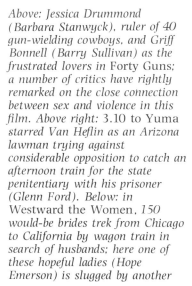

Above: Jessica Drummond (Barbara Stanwyck), ruler of 40 gun-wielding cowboys, and Griff Bonnell (Barry Sullivan) as the frustrated lovers in Forty Guns; *a number of critics have rightly remarked on the close connection between sex and violence in this film. Above right:* 3.10 to Yuma *starred Van Heflin as an Arizona lawman trying against considerable opposition to catch an afternoon train for the state penitentiary with his prisoner (Glenn Ford). Below: in* Westward the Women, *150 would-be brides trek from Chicago to California by wagon train in search of husbands; here one of these hopeful ladies (Hope Emerson) is slugged by another*

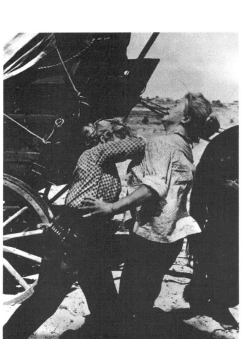

appearing in only one previous Western, *Destry Rides Again* (1939). Alan Ladd and James Cagney, previously identified with the gangster or thriller genre, made their mark: Alan Ladd's Shane provided one of the archetypal Western heroes of the decade, and the triumphant revival of Cagney's career began with an off-beat Western, Nicholas Ray's *Run for Cover* (1955). Veteran character actors like Walter Brennan and Andy Devine were much in demand, along with a new generation of 'heavies' including Dan Duryea, Richard Boone and Jack Elam. Young, up-and-coming actors were often teamed with older established stars, for example, Jeffrey Hunter with John Wayne in *The Searchers* and with Robert Ryan in *The Proud Ones*, both in 1956, or Anthony Perkins with Henry Fonda in Anthony Mann's *The Tin Star* (1957).

Leading female stars also took to the saddle. Marlene Dietrich totally dominated Fritz Lang's *Rancho Notorious* (1952) although, according to Lang, she was not happy playing an older woman. Jean Arthur made a notable screen comeback as the homesteader's wife in *Shane*. Joan Crawford gave a suitably larger-than-life performance as the tough owner of a gambling saloon in *Johnny Guitar*. But for toughness and self-reliance no-one could rival Barbara Stanwyck, who emerged as a leading Western star during the mid-Fifties in such pictures as *Cattle Queen of Montana* (1954), *The Violent Men* (1955), *The Maverick Queen* (1956) – Republic's first film in the new 'Scope-like anamorphic 'Naturama' – and, most impressive of all, as the ruthless ranch boss of *Forty Guns* (1957), Sam Fuller's much underrated Western, appropriately filmed in black-and-white CinemaScope.

In the landmark year of 1950 there was a major upgrading of the Western genre. John Ford directed *Rio Grande* (the last of his cavalry trilogy) and *Wagonmaster*. This superb tribute to the pioneers who travelled west in wagon trains drew on Ford's stock company of favourite actors, including Ward Bond, Jane Darwell, Russell Simpson, Ben Johnson and Harry Carey Jr.

Another veteran director, Henry King, produced an unexpected bonus from his collaboration with Gregory Peck, sandwiched between the prestige productions of *Twelve O'Clock High* (1949) and *David and Bathsheba* (1951). The theme of the gunslinger unable to live down his past has often been dealt with since, but never more effectively than in *The Gunfighter*, from 20th Century-Fox. Along with

Broken Arrow, it represented a natural extension of Darryl Zanuck's emphasis on the problem picture during the late Forties, which was here combined with his special interest in Americana.

The year 1950 also marked the debut of a number of new Western stars, and directors such as Anthony Mann and Delmer Daves. Mann directed his first three Westerns in 1950: *The Furies*, at Paramount, starring Barbara Stanwyck and Walter Huston; *Winchester '73*, at Universal, with James Stewart in his first mature Western role; and, at MGM, *Devil's Doorway*, in which Robert Taylor played an Indian fighting for the rights of his people. In Delmer Daves' *Broken Arrow*, Stewart played an Indian-scout who falls in love with and marries an Indian girl; Jeff Chandler played Cochise in this first modern Western to portray the Indians with human stature and dignity. William Wellman's

---

Shane was the box-office front-runner, but Mann's Westerns outdrew all opponents with the critics, especially in France

---

Across the Wide Missouri (1951), with Clark Gable, presented an intelligent treatment of the theme of a white trapper and his Indian wife which, although released in a badly shortened version, did well at the box-office.

However, the claim for a new respectability for the Western was firmly established in 1952 with the phenomenal success of *High Noon*. Its director, Fred Zinnemann, said:

'From the time Stanley Kramer and Carl Foreman told me the outline of the story, I saw this film *not* as a comment on the American Western hero, but as an enormously important contemporary theme which happened to take place in a Western setting.'

The tightly constructed script provided Gary Cooper with one of the best roles of his career (and his second Oscar).

The revival of Westerns by 1952 was reflected in their prominence among the top hits of that year. *High Noon* was closely followed in the box-office stakes by *Son of Paleface*, with Bob Hope, and Anthony Mann's *Bend of the River*, which marked a further advance in his collaboration with James Stewart. Raoul Walsh's *Distant Drums*, again with

Gary Cooper, and three pictures from MGM – William Wellman's *Westward the Women*, *Lone Star* with Gable, and *The Wild North* – all recorded distributors' rentals of over $2 million. But *Shane*, with rentals of over $8 million the following year, was the biggest Western hit of the decade. The fine cast was headed by Alan Ladd, Jean Arthur, Van Heflin and Brandon de Wilde, with Jack Palance as the villainous hired gun brought in to intimidate the homesteaders. The director, George Stevens, was ably supported by A.B. Guthrie's fine script and the Oscar-winning Technicolor camerawork of Loyal Griggs.

Among the many Westerns filmed in the new processes, Robert Aldrich had a big hit in 1954 with *Vera Cruz*, one of the first films in SuperScope. And although Anthony Mann proved in *The Far Country* (1954) that it was still possible to get excellent results from the old format, he finally made the transition to CinemaScope with *The Man From Laramie* (1955), the last of his films with Stewart; all of his subsequent Westerns were in 'Scope. Similarly, John Ford's masterpiece, *The Searchers* (1956), benefited from the superior photographic quality of VistaVision. The picture presents a harsher, more

bitter and sophisticated view of the West than is found in his earlier films.

The black-and-white picture made a temporary comeback during the late Fifties with Delmer Daves' *3.10 to Yuma* (1957) and Arthur Penn's *The Left-Handed Gun* (1958) starring Paul Newman. Both films presented sophisticated and realistic treatments of traditional themes – the lone lawman bringing an outlaw to justice, the story of Billy the Kid – with a modern emphasis on character and relationships on a small scale. The moments of violence develop naturally out of the intensity of personal conflict. Appropriately enough, *The Left-Handed Gun* was in the true Warners tradition of hard-hitting black-and-white pictures featuring a tough hero who dies a violent death in the final reel.

Warners was also responsible for one outstanding Western which brought the decade to a close, Howard Hawks' *Rio Bravo* (1959). Reflecting Hawks' dislike of *High Noon*, the picture may appear conventional on the surface; yet the characters and relationships are observed with great insight and wit while retaining the kind of vitality and spontaneity found in Hawks' earlier pictures:

'I determined to go back and try to get a little of the spirit we used to make pictures with. In *Rio Bravo* I imagine there are almost as many laughs as if we had started out to make a comedy.'

Hawks neatly built on the juxtaposition of old, established Westerners like John Wayne and Walter Brennan with a newer generation represented by Dean Martin and Angie Dickinson. And if the Wayne-Dickinson relationship, a mature man trying to cope with an independent-minded, tough-talking girl, recalls the Bogart-Bacall films of the Forties, this is not surprising, since Hawks was collaborating with two of his favourite scriptwriters from this period, Leigh Brackett and Jules Furthman.

Unfortunately, as the decade drew to a close those qualities developed by directors such as Daves, Boetticher and Hawks during the late Fifties were largely forgotten, and the studios increasingly turned to the overblown, blockbuster Western in the tradition of William Wyler's *The Big Country* (1958). The Sixties began rather unpromisingly with *The Alamo*, *The Magnificent Seven* – based on *Seven Samurai* – and a disappointing remake of *Cimmaron* (all 1960). These were followed by the scrappy *How the West Was Won* (1962), the first story picture in Cinerama. JOEL FINLER

Above left: Jack Palance as a hired gunfighter about to kill one of the settlers in Shane. *Above: a showgirl (Sophia Loren) in a touring theatrical troupe joins the gentlemen for a round of poker in George Cukor's* Heller in Pink Tights *(1960). Below, far left: in Broken Arrow Jeff Chandler played Cochise for the first but not the last time. Below left: the sheriff (John Wayne) makes his evening patrol in* Rio Bravo. *Below: Glenn Ford and Shirley MacLaine star in George Marshall's* The Sheepman *(1958), a delightful send-up of the archetypal range-war between sheepmen and cattlemen*

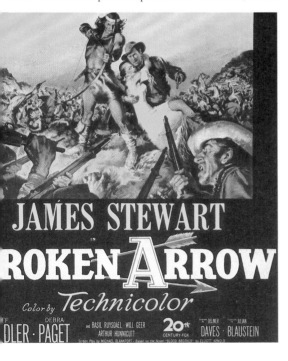

HIS ONLY FRIEND WAS HIS GUN...

HIS ONLY REFUGE – A WOMAN'S HEART!

GREGORY PECK IN THE Gunfighter

Helen WESTCOTT Millard MITCHELL Jean PARKER HENRY KING NUNNALLY JOHNSON

KARL MALDEN SKIP HOMEIER ANTHONY ROSS VERNA FELTON ELLEN CORBY RICHARD JAECKEL WILLIAM BOWERS & WILLIAM SELLERS William Bowers and Andre de Toth

20 CENTURY-FOX

Directed by Henry King, 1950
Prod co: 20th Century-Fox. **prod:** Nunnally Johnson. **sc:** William Bowers, William Sellers, from a story by William Bowers and Andre De Toth. **photo:** Arthur Miller. **ed:** Barbara McLean. **art dir:** Lyle R. Wheeler, Richard Irvine. **mus:** Alfred Newman. **r/t:** 84 minutes.
Cast: Gregory Peck (*Jimmy Ringo*), Helen Westcott (*Peggy Walsh*), Millard Mitchell (*Marshall Mark Strett*), Jean Parker (*Molly*), Mae Marsh (*Mrs O'Brien*), Karl Malden (*Mac*), Skip Homeier (*Hunt Bromley*), Anthony Ross (*Charlie*), Verna Felton (*Mrs Pennyfeather*), Ellen Corby (*Mrs Devlin*), Richard Jaeckel (*Eddie*), Alan Hale Jr (*first brother*), David Clarke (*second brother*), John Pickard (*third brother*), D.G. Norman (*Jimmy*), Angela Clarke (*Mac's wife*), Cliff Clark (*Jerry Marlowe*), Jean Inness (*Alice Marlowe*), Eddie Ehrhart (*Archie*), Albert Morin (*Pablo*).

to certain death in the bombing raids of *Twelve O'Clock High* (1949). King has often seemed a director better than his assignments, but in *The Gunfighter* he had a project that perfectly matched his essential modesty and directness of understatement. There is a tightness and a tension to this small, black-and-white film that is admirably and efficiently developed without mannerism and, in particular contrast to *Shane* without self-importance.

There is, of course, a' sub-theme to the film: one of particular relevance in the United States in 1950. It had to do with betrayal. The Peck character, though he had surely done bad things, was not a bad man. As much as anything, he was undone by a shift in the values of respectable society. In other words, he had been honoured for his deadly skill at his deadly trade when nice people had need of him to fight their battles for them. Now that they no longer require his services they will not come to his aid as he seeks peace from continued professional challenges. In the end he

dies precisely because his friends and neighbours turn him out and place him back on the road that can only lead to oblivion. Perhaps this was a metaphorical expression of contempt for the way that Hollywood in particular, and American society in general, was, at the moment of the film's release, turning against prominent leftists who, only a few years before, had seemed to be speaking for generally held liberal values and now found themselves alone and deserted by people who had once stood behind them. It is, of course, one of the values of *The Gunfighter* that it does not insist on this point – thus contrasting with *High Noon*'s heavy-handed harping on a similar parallel – and can be enjoyed simply as a well-made, highly professional genre exercise.

RICHARD SCHICKEL

Below: the director Henry King prepares the reunion scene, where Jimmy Ringo finally gets to see his wife, with Gregory Peck and Helen Westcott

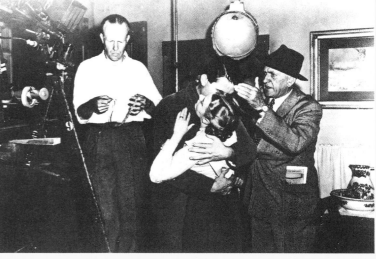

Like the celebrated but not necessarily more memorable Westerns that came immediately after it – *High Noon* (1952), *Shane* (1953), *Rio Bravo* (1959) – *The Gunfighter* was a highly self-conscious film. It quite knowingly took up and restated themes that had been present in this genre almost from the beginning and subtly indicated, here and there, that its makers knew that they were doing so. As a result, a film that might have been dismissed as a cliché became a work that the knowledgeable public – and reviewers – could embrace for its classicism without spoiling the groundlings' fun.

The theme is that old favourite, the reluctant gunman – a man fecklessly trying to outrun his unwanted reputation as a fast hand with a six-shooter. He discovers, in the course of the film, that even his home town, where his estranged wife is raising his son not to know who his father is, will not offer him protection from his past. He carries with him the Western loner's most basic dream of the little ranch far, far away where he can settle down at last, as well as the loner's hope that he can pass through streets and bar-rooms unrecognized by the kids and punks who want to make their reputations by beating him to the draw.

In short, the film covers familiar

country. Why, then, does *The Gunfighter* linger so pleasingly in the memory? One reason is its excellent dialogue. When Eddie threatens the weary Jimmy Ringo, the latter's contempt is crisply stated: 'Why don't you button up your breeches,' he advises the youth, 'and go home.' Later, when he is discussing the discrepancy between his fame and his fortune, he sadly reflects: 'Here I am, 35, and I ain't even got a good watch.' There is a homeliness in his speech, as befits his time and place, but a certain freshness and unexpectedness in it, too. Throughout the film Gregory Peck is laconic without lapsing into inarticulateness and, for once, he gets to make his point without having to make a speech. He responds almost gratefully to this opportunity to play integrity without having to talk about it endlessly.

Indeed the decency of that Lincolnesque image of his, which he cannot help but drag with him from film to film, provides a curious subtext against which to play a character who is, at bottom, a murderer for hire. Peck plays this contrast without overplaying it. The austere, not to say stark, *mise-en-scène* derives from the veteran director Henry King, for whom Peck created his other memorable performance, that of the American officer breaking under the strain of sending his fliers

2

4

Jimmy Ringo, a well-known gunfighter, walks into a bar where Eddie, a young hot-head trying to impress his friends, challenges him to a draw (1). Ringo is forced to kill him. He leaves town, meets Eddie's three brothers who are seeking revenge, disarms them and rides on.

He arrives in Cayenne where he meets Mark Strett, a former member of his gang, now the town marshal. Strett asks him to leave town, but Ringo says that he has come to see his wife Peggy and son Jimmy whom he has not seen for eight years. No-one except Strett and an old friend, Molly, knows that Peggy is Ringo's wife and Peggy has not even told her son that Ringo is his father.

While Strett goes to ask Peggy whether she will see Ringo, word gets around that a famous gunfighter is in town. Outside the saloon where Ringo is waiting, people gather – only to be shoo'd away periodically by the anxious bartender (2). Strett's mission is unsuccessful so Ringo asks Molly to intercede on his behalf (3).

While he waits for an answer, he is taunted by the town punk, Hunt Bromley (4), but Ringo frightens him off. Molly brings Peggy to meet Ringo (5); he begs her to come back to him, promising to keep out of trouble for a year and then send for her. He also sees his son again (6).

Meanwhile Eddie's brothers arrive in town (7). But just as they are about to shoot Ringo the marshal's deputy arrest them. As Ringo mounts his horse to leave town, Bromley catches him at a disadvantage and shoots him (8). Before he dies, Ringo asks Strett not to arrest Bromley but rather to leave him to the miseries of the life of a gunfighter (9).

6

9

The Ranown Cycle

Randolph Scott, a former romantic lead and long-established Western star, and the director Budd Boetticher, previously a bullfighter whose first job in movies was as a technical adviser on *Blood and Sand* (1941), made their first film together, *Seven Men From Now* in 1956. It was the beginning of an excellent series of cheaply made cowboy pictures that would definitely portray the Western hero as a dour, but strong and self-sufficient traveller through the barren terrain of life

'The Ranown cycle' is the designation critics have awarded a remarkable series of low-budget Westerns from the late Fifties, starring Randolph Scott and directed by Budd Boetticher: *Seven Men From Now* (1956), *The Tall T*, *Decision at Sundown* (both 1957), *Buchanan Rides Alone* (1958), *Ride Lonesome* (1959) and *Comanche Station* (1960).

The name is more evocative than precise. An acronym derived from *R*andolph Scott (star and associate producer) and Harry Joe Br*own* (producer or executive producer), 'Ranown' is not quite synonymous with Scott-Brown Productions, the partnership responsible for a line of bread-and-butter Westerns extending back to the late Forties. Moreover, *Seven Men From Now*, the film that brought Scott and Boetticher together – thereby qualifying as the first instalment in the cycle – did not involve Harry Joe Brown, but was made under the auspices of John Wayne's company, Batjac. To muddy the waters further, *Westbound* (1959), the sixth of the seven movies that Scott and Boetticher made in close succession, was strictly a contract job for Warner Brothers; it bears little formal or thematic resemblance to the others and is properly relegated to very marginal status.

When all this has been duly noted, 'the Ranown cycle' is an appropriately ringing appellation. Indeed, 'Ranown' sounds like just one more name for the character Scott played – with few but judicious variations – throughout the series: Stride, Brennan, Allison, Buchanan, Brigade and Cody. 'Cycle' is the right word, too; for markedly similar supporting characters, configurations of characters and dramatic situations and issues occur in each film – even the same creekside cottonwoods and lunar outcrops of desert rock, looking bleached and rounded as bone.

Most of the Ranown pictures describe journeys through open country, with the travellers sometimes pausing (but never lingering long) in towns. The two exceptions, *Decision at Sundown* and *Buchanan Rides Alone*, begin with the Scott character's arrival in a community and end with his departure from it. In all but two (*The Tall T* and *Buchanan Rides Alone*), he is a grim figure whose life has been consecrated to achieving justice for the violent death of his wife. (*Comanche Station* represents a slight variation in that the wife is presumed dead – by everyone but her husband – she having been carried off long ago by Indians.) His quests bring him into temporary contact and, usually, tenuous alliance with a small party of disreputable men, whose boss will support Scott against their common enemies (bad white men or Indians) but challenge him at that climactic moment when the course to Scott's entirely personal goal (revenge, the safe delivery of an innocent or the return of stolen goods) diverges from the leader's path to *his* ultimate goal (often reward money or the appropriation of stolen goods).

Both the Scott character and his unscrupulous ally know that this moment will come. Neither wants it – they often like each other in a peculiarly edgy way – but neither, given the integrity of character and personal resolve that interests Boetticher, can avoid a final confrontation. Boetticher had been a professional Matador before coming to Hollywood, and it is not hard to detect the rhythms of the *corrida* in the deadly, flirtatious style of encounter between these adversaries.

These rhythms inform each film as a whole. Boetticher's groups ride across changing terrain – desert wasteland one day, the beginnings of cow country the next day – and then sit down by camp-fires to pass uneasy nights. The small but carefully drawn population of these films meanders into criss-crossed conversational couplings: for example, Scott and the gang boss (splendidly played by the likes of Lee Marvin, Richard Boone, Pernell Roberts and Claude Akins); and the gang boss and his variously naive, jaded, gentle or sadistic companions (Henry Silva, Skip Homeier, L. Q. Jones, James Coburn, Richard Rust), with whom he often feels less rapport than with Scott. Other couplings include Scott and the woman who is always worked in somehow, sometimes with a less-than-manly husband in tow; and – a brilliantly directed sequence in the first and the last instalments of the series – Scott, the woman and the gang leader, who verbally makes love to the woman while affecting to discuss a theoretical sexual attraction. These are laconic colloquies, polished to a

...are, witty elegance by Boetticher and his best scriptwriter, Burt Kennedy (who worked on the screenplays of *Seven Men From Now*, *The Tall T*, *Ride Lonesome*, *Comanche Station*). Rare is the line of dialogue that does not drop a superfluous syllable in the interests of tightening the dramatic tension and hewing closer to the mythic Western vernacular.

The films' comedy is dry and black. It becomes most overt in *Buchanan Rides Alone*, a movie which Akira Kurosawa must have seen before making his samurai film *Yojimbo* (1961) subsequently remade by Sergio Leone as the Western *Per un Pugno di Dollari* (1964, *Fistful of Dollars*). Buchanan rides into the border community of Agrytown where everything – a steak, a bottle of whisky, a room – costs $10 and the corrupt Agry brothers enjoy rule of

law. Scott plays Buchanan in his broad-grinning, just-passin'-through, man-of-the-world mode. Almost by accident, he becomes involved in the life of the town when the Agrys set out to hang a wealthy young Mexican who has offended them.

Boetticher's directorial eye is dispassionate, distant and drily amused. He frames the action with an appreciation for clean lines and naturally expressive textures: the movement of figures across a landscape that is indifferent to justice, honour, morality; that is, finally, just a place where things happen, where life goes on with no meaning other than the sense of worth and purpose that strong individuals bring to it.

The Ranowns are at once the purest and most unassuming of great Westerns. They and their makers disdain messages, refuse to carry

Top: *Scott as Jefferson Cody, wounded in* Comanche Station. *Above left: Ben Stride, the grim-faced avenger, tracks down the men who murdered his wife. Above: Buchanan, the cocky hero, encounters the corruption of Agrytown and the brothers who run it*

the baggage of, for instance, the contemporary socio-political issues with which other Fifties film-makers felt obliged to 'elevate' this 'disreputable', 'commercial' genre. These unassuming B features with their sure sense of aesthetic self now loom over their pretentious contemporaries like the eternal rocks from which the protagonist of *Comanche Station* first appears, and into which he ultimately disappears at the end of the film.

RICHARD T. JAMESON

STANLEY KRAMER PRODUCTIONS presents

GARY COOPER

THERE IS NOTHING UNDER THE SUN
LIKE THE HIGH ADVENTURE OF "HIGH NOON"!

"HIGH NOON"

STANLEY KRAMER PRODUCTIONS presents GARY COOPER in HIGH NOON

HIGH NOON

Around 1950–51 the screenwriter Carl Foreman composed a scenario about an ageing marshal abandoned by his townsfolk and his bride and forced to stand alone against a team of gunmen. The rights of *The Tin Star*, a similar story by John W. Cunningham, were bought to avoid copyright litigation and production began on *High Noon* – a modest, low-budget, black-and-white Western that was to be the last of several collaborations between Foreman and independent producer Stanley Kramer. The director Fred Zinnemann, who had worked with them on *The Men* (1950), was signed and Gary

Cooper – at 51 a fading star – was cast as Will Kane, the hero.

It was the McCarthy era and Foreman, an alleged communist, had already clashed with the House Un-American Activities Committee. During the filming of *High Noon* he was subpoenaed but refused to name names or comment on his political persuasions – an action that reputedly won him the admiration of Gary Cooper, even though Cooper was a noted anti-communist and friendly witness. Foreman was eventually blacklisted, snubbed by Hollywood and obliged to continue his film career in Europe. It has since been fash-

ionable to emphasize the fact that *High Noon* is a bitter allegory of McCarthyism, with Kane as the hunted man who obeys his conscience and the cowardly people of Hadleyville as the American public that turned a blind eye to the witch-hunts. At the end of the film Kane, having dispatched his assailants, drops his marshal's badge into the dust – supposedly Foreman's way of showing how highly he regarded American justice and society.

Despite this, however, the action on the screen allows no time for the audience to worry about allegorical content. *High Noon* is confined to 85 minutes in the life of the small town, beginning around 10.35 on the morning of Kane's wedding and proceeding to just after 12.00. It consists of Kane's agonizing wait for his pursuers to arrive on the noon train, the intolerably tense and protracted gunfight in which every blind corner and alleyway promises a bullet in the stomach for the lone marshal, and the brief ending when he holds his wife in his arms and turns his back on the town. The accent on time running out for Kane is clearly stated by frequent close-ups of ticking clocks that bring noon tantalizingly nearer and give vocal and visual expression to the torturous heart-beat pulse of the story.

The ticking stabs at Kane, brilliantly played by Cooper. There is no mistaking how afraid the marshal is: his walk down the sun-beaten streets becomes increasingly mannered and stiff as time leaks away, but it acquires a strange and impressive resoluteness that stems less from ignorant courage than from a refusal to give in to the sickening fear within. At one point he goes into his office and buries

his head in his hands, sobbing. However this momentary capitulation is only an admission of mortality. It is a suggestion of weakness that merely emphasizes how resilient the man is, for soon afterwards he destroys his enemies – even if his wife has to lend a hand.

Similarly in *Shane* (1953), the hero buys a soda-pop in front of jeering cowboys in the store, displaying a misleading humility against which to contrast the deadly ability of his fists and gun. Both Kane and Shane were central figures in the new adult Western of the Fifties, their colossal reserves of courage and strength being occasionally at odds with characteristics like fear, pacifism and gentleness.

Kane must – and does – overcome not only his friendlessness and fear of death, but also the mortifying desertion by Amy, his bride of a few minutes. After the preview of *High Noon* met with a disappointing response, Kramer asked the composer Dmitri Tiomkin to write a song for the film. He came up with 'Do Not Forsake Me, Oh My Darlin'', an aching ballad which was added to the soundtrack to bridge various scenes. With its throbbing tune and recurring line of desperation – 'What will I do if you leave me?' – as if addressed by Kane to Amy, it provides a chilling motif, ebbing away at moments of despair to suggest the real reason for the torment etched on Kane's face.

In reality Gary Cooper had an ulcer at the time and was in considerable pain throughout filming. In contributing to Kane's tightlipped wretchedness it also helped Cooper to a second Oscar and revived his career as a Western star. The film also won Oscars for Best Song, Best Score and Best Editing and was a massive box-office success.

Political allegory, suspenseful psychological Western or apotheosis of nervous heroism, *High Noon* is, by any standards, a work of enduring excellence and its depiction of Will Kane patrolling the Hadleyville main street is one of the most memorable images from American cinema.

GRAHAM FULLER

Directed by Fred Zinnemann, 1952
Prod: Stanley Kramer. **sc:** Carl Foreman, loosely based on the story *The Tin Star* by John W. Cunningham. **photo:** Floyd Crosby. **ed:** Elmo Williams. **ass ed:** Harry Gerstad. **art dir:** Rudolph Sternad. **mus:** Dmitri Tiomkin. **song:** 'Do Not Forsake Me Oh My Darlin'' by Dmitri Tiomkin, Ned Washington, sung by Tex Ritter. **sd:** Jean Speak. **ass dir:** Emmett Emerson. **r/t** 85 minutes.
Cast: Gary Cooper (*Will Kane*), Thomas Mitchell (*Jonas Henderson*), Lloyd Bridges (*Harvey Pell*), Katy Jurado (*Helen Ramirez*), Grace Kelly (*Amy Kane*), Otto Kruger (*Percy Mettrick*), Lon Chaney (*Martin Howe*), Henry Morgan (*William Fuller*), Ian Macdonald (*Frank Miller*), Eve McVeagh (*Mildred Fuller*), Harry Shannon (*Cooper*), Lee Van Cleef (*Jack Colby*), Bob Wilke (*James Pierce*), Sheb Woolley (*Ben Miller*), Tom London (*Sam*), Ted Stanhope (*station master*), Larry Blake (*Gillis*), William Phillips (*barber*), Jeanne Blackford (*Mrs Henderson*), James Milligan (*baker*), Cliff Clark (*weaver*), Ralph Reed (*Johnny*), William Newell (*drunk*), Lucien Prival (*bartender*), Guy Beach (*Fred*), Howland Chamberlin (*hotel clerk*), Morgan Farley (*minister*), Virginia Christine (*Mrs Simpson*), Virginia Farmer (*Mrs Fletcher*), Jack Elam (*Charlie*), Paul Dubov (*Scott*), Harry Harvey (*Coy*), Tim Graham (*Sawyer*), Nolan Leary (*Lewis*), Tom Greenway (*Ezra*), Dick Elliott (*Kibbee*), John Doucette (*Trumbull*).

9

At 10.35 on a hot June morning in 1865 Will Kane, marshal of Hadleyville, marries a Mormon girl Amy (1). News immediately arrives that Frank Miller – an outlaw convicted by Kane five years earlier – has been pardoned, released from jail and is returning to seek revenge (2).

Although Kane has announced his retirement and is under no obligation to stay, he decides that it is his duty to protect the town from Miller and his three gunmen who are already waiting for their leader up at the station. However, Amy's religion has taught her to deplore violence and she tells Kane she is leaving on the noon train.

Going to the saloon and church to drum up support Kane finds that no-one is prepared to join forces with him (3). Everyone has an excuse for not fighting Miller, including the mayor and Kane's jealous deputy Harvey – beaten in a fight with the marshal when he tries to prevent Kane making a lone stand (4). Helen, Harvey's girl and a former lover of both Kane and Miller, vents her disgusted anger on the deputy (5) and decides to leave him and Hadleyville.

At noon the train brings Miller to Hadleyville (6). Kane – bruised, frightened and alone – prepares to take on the four men (7). He does not know that Amy, counselled by Helen (8), has remained in town. A running gunfight takes place in the streets, stables and on the sidewalks (9) and Amy at last helps her husband by shooting one of the gunmen. (10).

Kane manages to kill the other three. Embracing Amy (11) he flings his badge in the dust (12) and the couple ride away on a buckboard.

Lonesome Cowboy

Drifter, saddletramp, ghost rider – the wanderer in the wilderness who became the classic Western hero

He rides alone, entering the film behind th[e] main titles and departing – if still alive – at 'Th[e] End'. The movie belongs to him: the world tha[t] it shows would have remained unseen if n[ot] for his coming, and by his passing-throug[h] that world has been deeply affected. Yet h[e] cannot linger, for *he* does not belong. Someon[e] may be grateful to him for what he has don[e,] may love him, implore him to stay. He canno[t.] He has seen things, perhaps done things, tha[t] will not let him be at rest. Although he ma[y] have helped defend it, civilization has no plac[e] for him. Indeed, there may be no place for hi[m] among the living.

Silent knights

The 'lonesome cowboy' has been a mainstay [of] the Western genre for nearly as long as th[e] genre has been around; such early silent-fil[m] examples as Harry Carey and William S. Ha[rt] were 'good badmen' who rode on the shad[y] side of the law but could be relied upon [to] throw in their lot – and their lethal expertis[e] with firearms – with the cause of decenc[y] whenever a fair heroine was in jeopard[y.] During the early decades of sound film, th[e] figure was mostly watered down to become th[e] amiable drifter, benignly curious about wh[at] lay over the next hill. When he did sugge[st] some of the sinister shading of the Carey/Ha[rt] figure, he usually proved to be some kind [of]

66

distance, is precisely framed by the antlers of a deer the boy was aiming at with his toy gun; the director Stevens brings a similar mythic concentration to his compositions throughout the movie, reinforcing the sense that this is to be *the* definitive Western.

Shane describes himself to the Starretts as a man who drifts 'here and there – somewhere I've never been'. He stays at their farm partly out of recognition that they need his help, and partly out of a longing for a settled existence. Ultimately he realizes that he cannot escape his identity as a gunman, and that he has become as destructive an anachronism in the new West as the once admirable pioneer Riker (Emile Meyer), who has hardened into a robber-baron determined to drive the homesteading families out of 'his' valley. Shane destroys the Starretts' enemies in a veritable *Götterdämmerung*, but there is an overriding suggestion that he has taken a mortal wound himself; he rides out of the valley with Joey

Above: James Stewart as Will Lockhart, the lonely avenger in The Man From Laramie, *confronts the gun-runner (Arthur Kennedy) whose illicit trade has caused the death of Lockhart's brother at the hands of an Apache. Right: Charles Bronson, reticent and single-minded as the Man With the Harmonica in the mythical* Once Upon a Time in the West

secret agent who only wanted to look mysterious in order to infiltrate and get the goods on some nefarious gang.

The Fifties saw a change. The post-World War II Western was in general a more complex genre than the pre-war model. *Film noir* had extended its inky tendrils into the clear-water, big-sky landscapes of the Western, stylistically and spiritually: Western heroes and heroines could have passions as intense and peculiar as those of the villains; scenic backdrops that had once loomed as uncomplicatedly heroic analogues of the Westerner's strength, serenity and moral probity now looked gnarled and tortuous in the most dramatic cross-light a low-slanting sun could supply. Accordingly, the lone rider took on new colorations – moral, ethical, psychological, social, political – and new burdens of thematic complexity.

Out of the past

The new fashion in Western heroes can be appreciated clearly from a comparison of two great Fifties Westerns and their highly classical protagonists: George Stevens' *Shane* (1953), with Alan Ladd in the title role, and John Ford's *The Searchers* (1956), starring John Wayne as Ethan Edwards. Shane and Ethan both ride out of the wilderness and present themselves at an isolated homestead under threat of attack – by land barons and hostile

Left: in The Gunfighter *(1950) Gregory Peck played 'the fastest gun in the West' as a lonely fugitive haunted by the reputation that has cost him a place in society. Far left: William S. Hart, silent prototype of the Western nomad. Top left: Joey (Brandon de Wilde) and his father (Van Heflin) greet the stranger (Alan Ladd) who will change their lives in* Shane. *Above left: the revenge-hero Vern Haskell (Arthur Kennedy) stands on the left and apart from the social group (Stuart Randall, Marlene Dietrich, Francis McDonald, Jack Elam) in* Rancho Notorious

Indians, respectively. Each man has a violent past whose precise details remain evocatively mysterious to those they befriend and, indeed, to the audience as well. Each displays, through covert gesture and longing gaze, an unspoken love for a woman who can never be his – the homesteader's wife, Mrs Starrett (Jean Arthur) in *Shane*, Martha (Dorothy Jordan) in *The Searchers*. In the course of each film, the protagonist unofficially adopts a young pupil figure – Joey Starrett (Brandon de Wilde), Martin Pawley (Jeffrey Hunter) – whom he instructs in the ways of the world. Finally, each man intervenes decisively in the life of the jeopardized community, facing a dark adversary – Shane's is the hired gunfighter Wilson (Jack Palance), Ethan's the savage Chief Scar (Henry Brandon) – who is in some ways his counterpart; they prevail over these enemies and then turn away, receding from the newly stabilized civilization in the foreground to disappear into the same vastnesses of spiritual privacy from which they emerged.

The Shane myth

As hero figure, Shane is the distillation of the classical Western adventurer, pure in heart, motive, and Aryan blondness (of feature and of fringed buckskin costume). He rides a horse but first appears from an angle that suggests he may have descended from the clouds – an angel unsullied by earthly particularity, including a first (or last?) name. When first noticed by Joey, his figure, appearing in the

calling out his (and his mother's) love, and is last seen angling up toward the horizon – passing through a graveyard.

The search for the self

Although he has come to be regarded as one of the most compelling characters in American cinema, Ethan Edwards of *The Searchers* is not explicitly programmed for mythic status in the manner of Shane. Shane's final crisis of character is largely a rhetorical gesture on Stevens' part, whereas Ethan is defined as a fiercely divided human being from his very introduction. Ford's justly famous opening – a black screen is suddenly split by light as a pioneer woman opens the door of her ranch-house, then leads the camera outdoors to discover a grim figure riding out of the desert – is powerfully ambiguous. That absolute blackness is at once the void surrounding the telling of this and any other story in the medium of light and shadow; the cool, safe, womb-like precincts of civilized life, as set against the wind-swept, sun-blasted wilderness; and the darkness inside Ethan himself.

It becomes apparent (though not through dialogue) that Ethan has always loved his brother's wife; it is she who opens and stands in that doorway, she towards whom he is riding, she whom he can never reach. Martha Edwards will die horribly within 24 hours, and Ethan will chase her killers – and her captive daughter, Debbie – for years afterward. Yet in pursuing the dark Indians he is really chasing

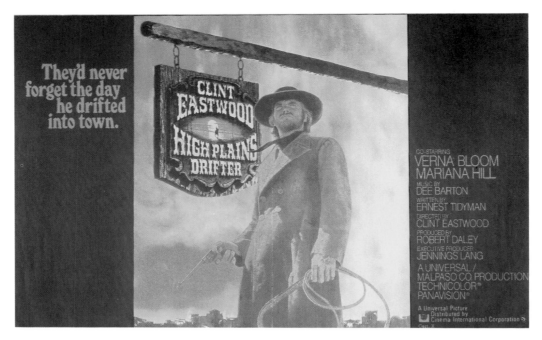

himself: the virulent racism he espouses is a projection of his own savage despair, the unconquerable sense of himself as an Other who can never have the home and contentment any man craves. At the climax of the film he must overcome this racism or destroy his niece (by then the bride of a Comanche), the one surviving vestige of all he has loved. He saves her; but the conclusion of the film shows Debbie being assimilated into another Western home, a brave community at the edge of civilization, while another door closes against Ethan and returns the screen to blackness.

The avengers
Ethan Edwards is in every way a darker hero than Shane, and the most poetically forceful example of the tortured protagonist encountered in so many Fifties Westerns. Most of Anthony Mann's Western heroes pursue revenge quests after a man who has shattered the tranquility of their former existence, but ultimately their struggle is to purge themselves of a personal violence that estranges them from loved ones, community, and all hope of a settled future. In films like *Winchester '73* (1950), *Bend of the River* (1952), *The Naked Spur* (1953) and *The Man From Laramie* (1955), Mann's characters make it, at least implicitly but Fritz Lang's

Top: Eastwood's parody of the 'stranger-in-town' theme has him as a ghost whose bloody revenge includes painting the town in question red – literally. Below: Jason Robards Jr as the doomed loner in The Ballad of Cable Hogue. *Below right: the departure of Shane*

bravura Western *Rancho Notorious* (1952) keeps faith with his Teutonic revenge epic *Die Nibelungen* (1924) in seeing the avenger (Arthur Kennedy) re-enacting the moral wrongs done him and being consumed in the process.

Nicholas Ray's *Johnny Guitar* (1954) and Samuel Fuller's *Run of the Arrow* (1957) define their loners in relation to the emerging society of the post-Civil War period; in both cases, the directors are really concerned with the American society of their own day rather than that of the 1860s. Johnny Guitar (Sterling Hayden) clings to the role of 'stranger' to defend against involvement in either the business and personal life of Vienna (Joan Crawford), the woman he once loved, or the machinations of the McCarthy-like establishment figures (played by Mercedes McCambridge and Ward Bond) who try to use the law to purge their town of an alien element (and unwanted competition). The communal crisis is resolved after much flamboyant action, and Johnny seems satisfactorily accommodated in a new love-relationship with his old flame – but the film's final images suggest that the couple will only find contentment apart from the hypocritical, if chastened, community.

O'Meara (Rod Steiger), the protagonist of *Run of the Arrow*, is an unregenerate Rebel who fired the last bullet in the War and, unwilling to be welcomed back into the Union, heads west with the outrageous notion of becoming a Sioux. Made at the time of the first turbulent civil-rights struggles, Fuller's movie is a clear allegory of an America that must accept its

ferociously mixed heritage and mixed bloo█ and face the future as one nation. Aft█ becoming involved in an Indian war, O'Mear█ ruefully accepts that he cannot run away fro█ being a white American, and departs with h█ Indian bride and adopted son to rejoin h█ brethren under the Stars and Stripes. Th█ outcome of this return to the United States█ not disclosed – Fuller's end title reads 'The en█ of this story can only be written by YOU' – bu█ the fact that the loner is the head of a racial█ mixed family bodes well symbolically.

New drifts
The modifications of the Fifties were to b█ extended in the Westerns of succeeding de█ ades, with the lonesome-cowboy figure b█ coming an increasingly stylized ingredient █ the genre itself became more and more e█ oteric. The ultra-allegorical *Lonely Are th█ Brave* (1962) focuses on a working cowhan█ (Kirk Douglas) who clings to his anachronist█ drifter's code in the face of modern-day reg█ mentation and mechanization, and is ult█ mately destroyed for it. Sam Peckinpah's We█ terns *Ride the High Country* (1962), *The Ballad █ Cable Hogue* (1970) and *Junior Bonner* (197█ likewise employ intransigent loners to mour█ the replacement of old codes of individu█ integrity with colourless socio-econom█ systems.

In the Italian Westerns of Sergio Leone, th█ lone rider becomes a black-comedy grotesqu█ flung in the face of conventional morality. Th█ Man With No Name (Clint Eastwood) in *Per u█ Pugno di Dollari* (1964, *Fistful of Dollars*), P█ *Qualche Dollari in Più* (1966, *For a Few Dolla█ More*), and *Il Buono, il Brutto, il Cattivo* (196█ *The Good, the Bad, and the Ugly*) is a bount█ hunter who murders without remorse (thoug█ not quite indiscriminately) – a running joke o█ the new amorality of the Sixties. The myst█ rious Man With the Harmonica (Charles Bron█ son) in Leone's *C'era una Volta il West* (196█ *Once Upon a Time in the West*) and Eastwood█ avenging gunman in his own film *High Plai█ Drifter* (1973)` carry the figure as far int█ lonesomeness as he can go. Each is a man wh█ is not a man at all, but a ghost returned t█ square accounts among the living. Bronson█ revenge scenario conspires nicely in perfectin█ the legend of the West, clearing the way for █ visionary epic of progress; Eastwood's is mo█ perverse – he will not be satisfied until he h█ remade and redubbed the world as He█ Having done so, he rides away – but where█

RICHARD T. JAMESO█

Three years after the American Civil War, Ethan Edwards returns to the home of his brother Aaron, sister-in-law Martha, their two daughters Lucy and Debbie and Martin Pawley (1). Lucy is affianced to Brad Jorgensen, whose family live nearby; his sister, Laurie, is in love with Martin.

Ethan, Captain the Reverend Clayton, Martin and the Texas Rangers ride out to recover some stolen cattle. While they are away, Chief Scar and his Comanche braves attack the Edwards' home. Ethan returns (2) to find that Aaron and Martha have been murdered and that the girls have been kidnapped.

The men embark on a search to find them and have to fight off an Indian attack. When Ethan comes upon Lucy's mutilated body, Brad Jorgensen goes mad with grief. He takes on the Comanches single-handed and is killed.

Ethan and Martin continue to hunt for Debbie. They endure hard winters (3), scorching summers (4) and assaults from white men and Indians. They finally track down Scar and his warriors (5) only to find that Debbie has become one of his squaws (6). She tells Ethan and Martin to leave without her. Ethan tries to kill her but Martin prevents him (7). The Comanches appear and Ethan is wounded fighting them off.

When Scar's new encampment is discovered, Ethan, Martin and the Rangers attack. Ethan finds that Scar has been killed by Martin, who has taken Debbie with him. Ethan scalps the dead chief (8), follows Martin and overpowers him. Just when it seems he is going to kill Debbie, he takes her in his arms (9).

The searchers take the girl back to the Jorgensens' farm. Martin is reunited with Laurie. Ethan lingers outside the door and then wanders off alone (10).

Directed by John Ford, 1956

Prod co: C.V. Whitney Pictures Inc/Warner Brothers. **exec prod:** Merian C. Cooper. **ass prod:** Patrick Ford. **sc:** Frank S. Nugent, from the novel by Alan LeMay. **photo** (Technicolor and VistaVision)**:** Winton C. Hoch, Alfred Gilks. **ed:** Jack Murray. **art dir:** Frank Hotaling, James Basevi, Victor Gangelin. **mus:** Max Steiner. **mus orch:** Murray Cutter. **song:** Stan Jones. **sd:** Hugh McDowell, Howard Wilson. **cost:** Frank Beetson, Ann Peck. **prod sup:** Lowell Farrell. **ass dir:** Wingate Smith. **r/t:** 119 minutes.
Cast: John Wayne (*Ethan Edwards*), Jeffrey Hunter (*Martin Pawley*), Vera Miles (*Laurie Jorgensen*), Ward Bond (*Captain the Reverend Samuel Clayton*), Natalie Wood (*Debbie Edwards*), John Qualen (*Lars Jorgensen*), Olive Carey (*Mrs Jorgensen*), Henry Brandon (*Chief Scar*), Ken Curtis (*Charlie McCorry*), Harry Carey Jr (*Brad Jorgensen*), Antonio Moreno (*Emilio Figueroa*), Hank Worden (*Mose Harper*), Lana Wood (*Debbie as a child*), Walter Coy (*Aaron Edwards*), Dorothy Jordan (*Martha Edwards*), Pippa Scott (*Lucy Edwards*), Pat Wayne (*Lieutenant Greenhill*), Bill Steele (*Ranger Nesbitt*), Cliff Lyons (*Colonel Greenhill*), Beulah Archuletta (*Look*), Jack Pennick (*private*), Peter Mamakos (*Futterman*), Chuck Roberson (*Texas Ranger*), Away Luna, Billy Yellow, Bob Many Mules, Exactly Sonnie Betsuie, Feather Hat Jr, Harry Black Horse, Jack Tin Horn, Many Mules Son, Percy Shooting Star, Pete Gray Eyes, Pipe Line Begishe, Smile White Sheep and other members of the Navajo tribe (*Comanches*).

Given the humour, warmth and nostalgia of John Ford's Westerns from *Stagecoach* (1939) to *Wagonmaster* and *Rio Grande* (both 1950), it seemed barely conceivable that he would allow the emergence of the 'psychological' Western in the early Fifties to affect his own roseate vision of the West. *The Searchers*, however, was to prove his most anguished and desperate work.

Whether or not Ford had been influenced by the new trend will never be known, but certainly before *The Searchers* none of his heroes had been permitted to disrupt the complacent celebration of the folk rituals by which he set so much store – at least, not to the extent that the populist philosophy behind them was questioned.

Ethan Edwards, the damned, anarchic hero of *The Searchers*, does just that. There is utter contempt for the customs that bind and

sustain society in the way that he cuts short the funeral of his murdered brother and sister-in-law – 'Put an Amen to it' – to begin his relentless pursuit of Scar and Debbie. Later returning home empty-handed midway through the quest, his arrival completely wrecks the wedding of Laurie Jorgensen and the insipid rancher Charlie McCorry. As a result of this intervention, Laurie resumes her long-distance romance with Martin Pawley, Ethan's fellow searcher. She thus forsakes the homesteader for the wanderer. Ethan is the agent of this treason, and through the film the audience travels with him – away from settlements and civilization – to the brink of the destruction of Ford's hitherto secure moral universe.

Virtually every gesture, every action in *The Searchers* mirrors or mocks Ethan's inner bitterness and

obsessions. There is the moment when his brother's wife, Martha, strokes Ethan's cape – a sad indication of their mutual but impossible love. Scar's later violation of Martha seems a perverted expression of Ethan's own frustrated sexual longing. In another scene, Ethan is highly amused when Martin unintentionally purchases a Comanche squaw, Look; this incident ironically functions as the comic obverse of Debbie's miscegenation with Scar, a union that fills Ethan with loathing for her.

The parched desert landscape across which Ethan and Martin trek is itself a metaphor for Ethan's self-denial and pointless, impotent endurance. The daunting monoliths and wide-open spaces of Monument Valley, the claustrophobic interiors of the cavalry outpost and the dark cave in which the searchers hide out, and the snowbound wastes of winter combine to create a nightmare terrain in which Ethan and Martin go round and round in circles, finally locating Scar and Debbie just a few miles from where they started.

The hunt is carried on in a deceptively relaxed manner; as it progresses, tension and unease mount insinuatingly, making for a breath-

taking climax when Ethan catches Debbie defenceless. Two truly terrifying close-ups of Ethan's face – one as he realizes that the Indians are attacking his brother's home, the other when he is confronted with white women who have gone mad after being held captive by Indians – have already indicated the ferocity of his intentions. The film's startlingly bright colours, the climatic extremes of hot and cold, and scenes like Ethan's needless slaughter of the buffalo help to convey his mental instability and the insane nature of his quest.

Calm is suddenly restored when Ethan lifts Debbie into his arms instead of killing her and then returns her safely to the Jorgensens. However, the film's main concern is not for her but for Ethan. Unlike Martin, who is free to settle down with Laurie, he has no place in a civilized, family-based community. Ford, having questioned his traditional values of order and stability, does not ultimately desert them: the final shot is of a door closing on Ethan, who is fated, like the spirit of the dead Indian whose eyes he shoots out earlier in the film, 'to wander forever between the winds'. His search has not ended and never can.   GRAHAM FULLER

John Wayne's long, final illness in the spring and summer of 1979 unleashed a tidal wave of American emotion. As the media constantly reminded everyone, Wayne was the man who carried 'true grit' over from the movie screen into real life: no self-respecting American could fail to be moved by the sight of the Duke, ravaged by 'Big C' but still a vast and imposing presence, looming up before the TV cameras at the 1979 Academy Awards ceremony. It *was* an awesome occasion:

'Oscar and I have something in common,' he said that night. 'Oscar first came to the Hollywood scene in 1928. So did I. We're both a little weatherbeaten, but we're still here and plan to be around for a whole lot longer.'

Two months later he was dead, but even as the old man slipped away Maureen O'Hara and Elizabeth Taylor fought desperately to win him a Congressional Medal of Honour, the highest tribute that can be paid to an American. It was the least President Carter could do, and the American people were able to take part in the medal-wearing too with the mass-minting of duplicate gold awards bearing the simple legend 'John Wayne, American'.

Above all others Wayne was the film star whom America had chosen as its symbol of strength, bravery, manliness, patriotism and righteousness in the post-war years. The film journalist Alexander Walker has persuasively argued in his book *Stardom* that Wayne 'was the most complete example of a star who has taken his politics into films and his films into public image'.

A Republican at Republic

The image of Wayne as the ultimate American fighting for right grew up during World War II when he played the war-hero in Republic's *Flying Tigers* (1942) and *The Fighting Seabees* (1944), and in the wake of Hiroshima when American military might was most in need of justification. In *Back to Bataan, They Were*

Above: the Duke in jovial mood on set for The Cowboys *(1972). Right: James Stewart, John Ford and Wayne pose for a publicity shot during the filming of* The Man Who Shot Liberty Valance. *Right, background: Colonel Marlowe waves farewell to his beloved after escaping from the Rebels by blowing up a bridge in* The Horse Soldiers

Marion Michael Morrison, a name to be conjured with – yet known by all. It is curious that women don't really take to him while men idolize him, and both will always see him sitting squarely on the back of a horse with a six-gun at his hip. However, given that as John Wayne he remained a superstar for over four decades, there must have been more to him than that . . . or must there?

Above left: pioneers (Marguerite Churchill and Wayne) take to The Big Trail (1930) in a realistic Western with 'grubby' actors. Above: Oliver Hardy and Wayne in The Fighting Kentuckian (1949), a tale of two men's fight to help French refugees settle in Alabama. Below: Sergeant Stryker (Wayne) leads an attack in The Sands of Iwo Jima

Expendable (both 1945), the fiercely jingoistic *The Sands of Iwo Jima* (1949), and John Ford's cavalry trilogy – *Fort Apache* (1948), *She Wore a Yellow Ribbon* (1949) and *Rio Grande* (1950) – he played war leaders who were tough, courageous, compassionate and *American*. Meanwhile, back at the Hollywood front Wayne, a staunch Republican and President of the Motion Picture Alliance for the Preservation of American Ideals, was taking an active part in running Communists out of the film capital – and colleagues out of their livelihood.

The films that also involved Wayne on the production side are those which most cohesively unite his movie and public images. *Big Jim McLain* (1952), which he co-produced, is pro-McCarthyist propaganda with Wayne as a tough HUAC investigator pursuing 'pinkos'; in *The Alamo* (1960), his first film as director, he played Davy Crockett defending Texas against Santa Anna's Mexican army – a martyr for American freedom; *The Green Berets* (1968) was his second stab at direction and is a vituperative pro-Vietnam War film in which he plays a mercenary routing the Vietcong. As 'pro-American' propaganda this is strong, sometimes unpalatable stuff, and he even recorded an LP called 'Why I Love America' with Robert Mitchum. Now there is a hint of bathos in that title, as there is in the whole of Wayne's over-inflated image as the last American hero, and it would be feasible to suggest that Wayne was aware of it. His Republicanism and anti-Communism (he had read widely

in Communist literature and in political science) were sincere, and he was a fervent supporter of Eisenhower, Goldwater and Nixon, but perhaps he knew too the power of talismen, bronze medals and movie images in the art of propaganda. Yet, strange as it may seem, in his greatest films Wayne's characters are not all that America would have them be.

South of the border . . .

If Wayne was and is a symbol of Americanism then, politically and socially, no other actor has done so much to undermine the self-righteous bluster of WASPish – White Anglo-Saxon Protestant – redneck values, both by espousing them and showing the neuroses nagging away at them. Wayne married three Spanish-Americans during his lifetime (so much for *The Alamo*) and eventually turned to Catholicism on his death-bed. If Ford, Hawks and the directors at Republic hadn't grabbed him for Westerns and war films in the late Forties and early Fifties, he might have been an effective star of *film noir*, so thoroughly ambiguous and troubled is his image when scrutinized. In fact Ford's *The Searchers* (1956) is a Western *film noir* with Wayne as a psychopath trapped in the alternatively light and dark landscape of his own mind. Even if Wayne *was* politically naive then surely he understood the dreadful frailty of his bloated, brow-beating characters and that the anger, insensitivity and spitefulness of Tom Dunson in *Red River* (1948), Sergeant Stryker in *The Sands of Iwo Jima* and Tom Doniphon in *The Man Who Shot Liberty Valance* (1962) showed the bully and the tyrant in the hero who defends his flag at all costs. These characters are tired, unhappy men, soured and warped by their own experiences and plunged into crises of conscience which they can only solve by blasting their way out.

For all their self-sufficiency and arrogant confidence Wayne's movie characters – his American heroes – are lonely, sulky, ill-

tempered and desperate. In good moods they tend to be bluff and patronizing – Wayne's grin is cracked, his eyes narrowed under his brow with suspicion. In bad moments they are monstrous; recall the incident in *Red River* when Dunson bounds across the trail, draws and shoots the cocky gunslinger without stopping his relentless march and lays into his young foster-son Matt (Montgomery Clift), a fury of flailing fists and mad temper. 'I never knew that big sonovabitch could act,' Ford said to Hawks after seeing *Red River*. As old men or neurotics Wayne was especially effective and knew exactly what he was about, as did Ford – his patron and mentor – and in *The Searchers*, *The Horse Soldiers* (1959), a wearied view of the Civil War, and *The Man Who Shot Liberty Valance*, they share the knowledge that the American Dream has become an American nightmare.

No Janet for John

On other levels Wayne's characters are equally ill at ease. It is significant that in many of his films he is essentially womanless. In *Red River* he leaves his girl behind (intending to return) but she is killed by Indians; *She Wore a Yellow Ribbon* finds him as a mawkishly sentimental widower who confides in his wife's grave; in *Rio Grande* he is estranged from his wife

Above left: ace Indian hunter Lt. Col. Kirby Yorke, who involves himself in the Apache war to protect the settlers in Rio Grande. *Above: Townsend Harris, a USA envoy sent to hostile Japan to arrange a trade treaty in* The Barbarian and the Geisha *(1958)*

because he burnt down her home in the Civ[il] War; in *The Searchers* the woman he loves i[s] married to his brother; *The Man Who Sho[t] Liberty Valance* sees him lose his girl to the ma[n] who also usurps his heroism. The Wayn[e] persona inevitably engenders sexual disha[r]mony. For such an American hero Wayn[e] frequently cut an impotent, asexual figure – s[o] colossal that he swamps mere masculinity. H[e] was certainly no Gable – after all, how man[y] women find the Duke attractive? – and this [is] surely not the way the American male likes t[o] view himself.

Of course there is an escape clause, fo[r] Wayne is seldom just a tyrant. After Dunso[n] and Matt have fought themselves into th[e] ground in *Red River*, Tess Millay (Joanne Dru[)] comes up to them: 'Whoever would hav[e] thought that you two could have killed eac[h] other?' she chides, and the loving father-so[n] relationship is re-established. 'Come o[n] Debbie, let's go home,' Ethan (Wayne) says [to] his niece instead of killing her as he had set ou[t]

Filmography

1927 The Drop Kick (uncredited) (GB: Glitter); Mother Machree (ass. prop man; +extra). **'28** Four Sons (ass. prop man); Hangman's House (uncredited). **'29** Words and Music; Salute; Men Without Women. **'30** Born Reckless (ass. prop man); Rough Romance; Cheer Up and Smile; The Big Trail. **'31** Girls Demand Excitement; Three Girls Lost; Men Are Like That (GB: The Virtuous Wife); The Deceiver; Range Feud; Maker of Men. **'32** The Voice of Hollywood No 13 (short) (announcer only); Shadow of the Eagle (serial); Texas Cyclone; Two-Fisted Law; Lady and Gent; The Hurricane Express (serial); The Hollywood Handicap (short) (guest); Ride Him Cowboy (GB: The Hawk); The Big Stampede; Haunted Gold. **'33** The Telegraph Trail; The Three Musketeers (serial; re-edited into feature Desert Command/ Trouble in the Legion, 1946); Central Airport; Somewhere in Sonora; His Private Secretary; The Life of Jimmy Dolan (GB: The Kid's Last Fight); Baby Face; The Man from Monterey;

Riders of Destiny; College Coach (GB: Football Coach); Sagebrush Trail. **'34** The Lucky Texan; West of the Divide; Blue Steel; The Man from Utah; Randy Rides Alone; The Star Packer; The Trail Beyond; The Lawless Frontier; 'Neath Arizona Skies. **'35** Texas Terror; Rainbow Valley; The Desert Trail; The Dawn Rider; Paradise Canyon; Westward Ho; The New Frontier; The Lawless Range. **'36** The Oregon Trail; The Lawless Nineties; King of the Pecos; The Lonely Trail; Winds of the Wasteland; The Sea Spoilers; Conflict. **'37** California Straight Ahead; I Cover the War; Idol of the Crowd; Adventure's End; Born to the West (reissued as Hell Town). **'38** Pals of the Saddle; Overland Stage Raiders; Santa Fe Stampede; Red River Range. **'39** Stagecoach; The Night Riders; Three Texas Steers (GB: Danger Rides the Range); Wyoming Outlaw; New Frontier; Allegheny Uprising (GB: The First Rebel). **'40** The Dark Command; Three Faces West; The Long Voyage Home; Seven Sinners (GB reissue title: Café of the Seven Sinners); Melody Ranch

Above: Wayne as a rancher enlisting the help of even small boys in The Cowboys *(1972). Above centre: a muddy reconciliation for* McLintock! *and estranged wife (Maureen O'Hara). Above right: Mattie (Kim Darby) and the marshal visit her father's grave in* True Grit.

do in *The Searchers*, and it was Jean-Luc Godard who pinpointed the secret of Wayne's appeal when he wrote, 'How can I hate John Wayne upholding Goldwater and yet love him tenderly when abruptly he takes Natalie Wood into his arms in the last reel of *The Searchers?*' Elizabeth Taylor was near the mark too when she said in that Congressional Medal plea, 'He was as tough as an old nut and soft as a yellow ribbon'.

Wayne was capable of an extraordinary gentleness and chivalry and Ford was early to spot this when he cast him as Ringo, an outlaw who treats the whore Dallas (Claire Trevor) like a lady, in *Stagecoach* (1939). True, he was more accustomed to giving a girl a slap on the behind – most often Maureen O'Hara ('She's a big, lusty, wonderful gal . . . my kinda gal') who as the shrewish colleen of *The Quiet Man* (1952) warrants a playful smack and as the wife in *McLintock!* (1963) a thrashing with a shovel, but tenderness often undercuts his chauvinism. O'Hara seemed the only female

capable of bringing out the erotic in Wayne – caught bare-legged with him in a graveyard during the thunderstorm in *The Quiet Man* she charges the air between them with sexual electricity – despite his having made three films with Dietrich. In *Three Godfathers* (1948) and *The Alamo* Wayne also showed a familiarity with babies and toddlers, but those scenes are best forgotten. Tenderness and warmth are an acceptable part of the noble savage's make-up; allowed to be maudlin Wayne was embarrassing to watch.

Ford's *Stagecoach* had caught the right mixture of gentleness and toughness, and even gives a glimpse of the uncertainty in the Wayne hero. The opening shot of Ringo twirling his rifle over his arm saluted his arrival as a star, but in fact Wayne was already a well-known face, albeit in B pictures.

Shooting to stardom
He was born Marion Michael Morrison in Winterset, Iowa, in 1907, the son of a druggist who took the family West to Glendale, Los Angeles, when Marion was nine. In 1925 he won a football scholarship to the University of Southern California where the Western star Tom Mix saw him. Mix offered him a job shifting props at Fox and there Wayne met John Ford who employed him as a herder of

geese on the set of *Mother Machree* (1927). He appeared as an Irish peasant in Ford's *Hangman's House* (1928) and received his first screen credit as Duke Morrison for a bit-part in *Words and Music* (1929).

Then Raoul Walsh found him, changed his name to John Wayne and made him grow his hair long for the part of the wagon-train scout in the epic Western *The Big Trail* (1930). However, the film failed and despite a studio build-up, Wayne was consigned to B Westerns at Columbia, Mascot, Monogram (for whom he made a series as Singin' Sandy beginning with *Riders of Destiny* in 1933) and eventually Republic on Poverty Row. But he kept in with Ford and was finally bullied by him into a starring career that lasted for forty years.

By the Sixties Wayne had become an American institution, too formidable a presence for the good of his films except when working with Ford or Hawks. The long-awaited Oscar came for his portrayal of Rooster Cogburn, the one-eyed war-horse in *True Grit* (1969), but it was a tribute to Wayne's long career rather than to that particular performance. With his last film, *The Shootist* (1976), man and myth became inseparable: the movie begins with a sequence of clips from old John Wayne movies, a requiem for the character he is playing – an ex-gunfighter dying of cancer – and for himself.

The giant's shadow remains
As movie stars go John Wayne is pretty well indestructible, being the survivor of some two hundred films. Even the uncovering of the darker side of his image seems to inflate him all the more, as did the cancer he subdued for so long. 'I hope you die,' Martin Pawley (Jeffrey Hunter) shouts in rage at Ethan in *The Searchers*. 'That'll be the day,' Ethan grins back. Like Ethan, Wayne endures and is here to stay whether he is wanted or not; a dubious American hero but undoubtedly a remarkable screen presence.

GRAHAM FULLER

uncredited). '41 A Man Betrayed (GB: Citadel of Crime); Lady from Louisiana; The Shepherd of the Hills. '42 Lady for a Night; Reap the Wild Wind; The Spoilers; In Old California; Flying Tigers; Reunion in France (GB: Mademoiselle France); Pittsburgh. '43 A Lady Takes a Chance; In Old Oklahoma. '44 The Fighting Seabees; Tall in the Saddle. '45 Flame of the Barbary Coast; Back to Bataan; They Were Expendable; Dakota. '46 Without Reservations. '47 Angel and the Badman (+prod); Tycoon. '48 Red River; Fort Apache; Three Godfathers. '49 Wake of the Red Witch; The Fighting Kentuckian (+prod); She Wore a Yellow Ribbon; The Sands of Iwo Jima. '50 Rio Grande. '51 Operation Pacific; The Bullfighter and the Lady (prod. only); Flying Leathernecks; Jet Pilot. '52 The Quiet Man; Big Jim McLain (+co-exec. prod). '53 Trouble Along the Way; Island in the Sky (+co-exec. prod); Hondo (+co-exec. prod). '54 The High and the Mighty (+co-exec. prod). '55 The Sea Chase; Blood Alley (+exec. prod). '56 The Con-

queror; The Searchers. '57 The Wings of Eagles; Legend of the Lost (+co-exec. prod). '58 I Married a Woman (guest); The Barbarian and the Geisha. '59 Rio Bravo; The Horse Soldiers. '60 The Alamo (+dir; +prod); North to Alaska. '62 The Comancheros (+add. dir, uncredited); Hatari!; The Man Who Shot Liberty Valance; The Longest Day; How the West Was Won *ep* The Civil War. '63 Donovan's Reef; McLintock! (+exec. prod). '64 Circus World (GB: The Magnificent Showman). '65 The Greatest Story Ever Told; In Harm's Way; The Sons of Katie Elder. '66 Cast a Giant Shadow (+co-exec. prod). '67 El Dorado; The War Wagon (+co-exec. prod). '68 The Green Berets (+co-dir; +exec. prod); Hellfighters. '69 True Grit; The Undefeated. '70 Chisum; Rio Lobo. '71 Big Jake (+exec. prod). '72 The Cowboys; Cancel My Reservation (guest). '73 The Train Robbers (+exec. prod); Cahill – United States Marshal (+exec. prod) (GB: Cahill). '74 McQ. '75 Brannigan (GB); Rooster Cogburn. '76 The Shootist.

the film recalls Hawks' *Only Angels Have Wings* (1939), scripted by Jules Furthman, about a group of flyers whom Cary Grant, as their leader, keeps on a steady course.

Furthman also worked on Josef von Sternberg's *Underworld* (1927) with its provocative gangster's moll called 'Feathers'; the character of the same name played by Angie Dickinson in *Rio Bravo* is initially viewed as a distraction but proves her worth. Even in the somewhat suspect casting of pop singer Ricky Nelson, Hawks not only allowed him to sing but found a use for it when the others in the group join in the song – or, in Wayne's case, observe benevolently – as an expression of team solidarity.

Hawks himself explained another way in which the relationships were subtly developed:

'Dean Martin had a bit in which he was required to roll a cigarette. His fingers weren't equal to it and Wayne kept passing him cigarettes. All of a sudden you realize that they are awfully good friends or he wouldn't be doing it.'

This was a piece of business worked out on the set.

The film was a comfortable success, revitalizing Hawks' career, although ten other 1959 releases did better on the North American market and it came out level at the box-office with Fred Zinnemann's *The Nun's Story*. Hawks continued to make films in similar vein, stronger on characters than in story. In *El Dorado* (1967) and *Rio Lobo* (1970) he even re-used the format of *Rio Bravo*, but with diminishing results.

Rio Bravo also influenced young film-makers, notably John Carpenter who updated its basic situation into a modern-day Los Angeles police station under siege in *Assault on Precinct 13* (1976) and acknowledged his indebtedness by editing the film under the pseudonym of 'John T. Chance', the name of the sheriff played by Wayne in *Rio Bravo*.
ALLEN EYLES

Rio Bravo has come to be accepted as a perfect example both of the Western genre and of the work of its director, Howard Hawks. It was not born with that reputation. 'Well-made but awfully familiar fare', declared A. H. Weiler in the *New York Times*. 'The film lasts almost as long as five TV Westerns laid end to end', drawled *Time* magazine. Arthur Knight in *The Saturday Review* saw further:

'As standard Western fare as has ever turned up on a Hollywood menu . . . But when brewed by Howard Hawks . . . suddenly everything begins to work. There is excitement, tension, the pleasure of looking at Western landscapes, and the age-old justification when the good guys beat the bad . . .'

It was nearly three years after the failure of his *Land of the Pharaohs* (1955) that Hawks resumed his career with *Rio Bravo*, shooting it in May–July 1958 with Old Tucson, Arizona, as the main location. Hawks decided to 'try and get a little of the spirit we used to make pictures with'; he was inspired, in a backhanded way, by Fred Zinnemann's *High Noon* (1952) which concerned a marshal confronted by revenge-seeking desperadoes. As Hawks noted in an interview with Peter Bogdanovich:

'Gary Cooper ran around trying to get help and no one would give him any. And that's rather a silly thing for a man to do, especially since at the end of the picture he is able to do the job by himself. So I said, we'll do just the opposite, and take a real professional viewpoint: as Wayne says when he's offered help, "If they're really good, I'll take them. If not, I'll just have to take care of them".'

High Noon may not have been the only Western that influenced Hawks. The central situation of a lawman holding a prisoner under siege had occurred strikingly in *3.10 to Yuma* (1957) and Walter Brennan had played a jail-keeper in another good Western, *The Proud Ones* (1956) which, like *Rio Bravo*, concerned the relationship between a marshal and his deputy.

However, Hawks deliberately emphasized characterization over plot in making *Rio Bravo*. He realized that television series had made most Western plots excessively familiar. Rather audaciously, Hawks and his screenwriters, Jules Furthman and Leigh Brackett, did little to develop the personalities of the villains, who were normally more colourful and extravagant than the heroes of Fifties Westerns – for instance, Jack Palance in *Shane* (1953). The prisoner, played by Claude Akins, is adequately established but not dwelt upon; and the men outside are even less individualized, notable only for their number. Instead, Hawks makes his key relationship that between John Wayne as sheriff and Dean Martin as the alcoholic deputy. The deputy's full recovery of self-esteem is the main story development. The old jail-keeper and the young gunhand played by Ricky Nelson complete a group united in their professionalism and loyalty towards each other. In this respect,

Directed by Howard Hawks, 1959
Prod co: Armada. **prod:** Howard Hawks. **sc:** Jules Furthman, Leigh Brackett, from a story by B. H. McCampbell. **photo** (Technicolor): Russell Harlan. **ed:** Folmar Blangsted. **art dir:** Leo K. Kuter. **cost:** Marjorie Best. **mus:** Dmitri Tiomkin. **lyr:** Paul Francis Webster. **sd:** Robert B. Lee. **ass dir:** Paul Helmick. **r/t:** 141 minutes.
Cast: John Wayne (*John T. Chance*), Dean Martin (*Dude*), Ricky Nelson (*Colorado Ryan*), Ward Bond (*Pat Wheeler*), Angie Dickinson (*Feathers*), Walter Brennan (*Stumpy*), John Russell (*Nathan Burdett*), Pedro Gonzalez-Gonzalez (*Carlos*), Estelita Rodriguez (*Consuela*), Claude Akins (*Joe Burdett*), Malcolm Atterbury (*Jake*), Harry Carey Jr (*Harold*), Bob Steele (*Matt Harris*), Bob Terhune (*bartender*), Ted White (*Bart*).

Dude, a former deputy in the Texas border town of Rio Bravo, has been disappointed in love and turns to drink, becoming the town's laughing-stock (1). He pulls himself together to help sheriff John T. Chance in arresting Joe Burdett for murder and gets another crack at his old job (2).

Joe's rancher brother, Nathan, bottles the town up tight while the cantankerous jail-keeper Stumpy (3) is ready to shoot Joe if any rescue attempt is made. Chance tries to order a gambling woman, Feathers, to leave town but she stays and befriends him (4). Chance's old friend Pat Wheeler arrives in town (5), offers help and is gunned down by Nathan's men. Chance is taken by surprise on Main Street and rescued by Feathers and by Colorado, Wheeler's young gunhand (6), who becomes a deputy (7). Dude is captured by Nathan Burdett and Chance agrees to a trade. But Dude leaps on Joe as they pass each other in the exchange and the two sides shoot it out.

Chance's team uses dynamite to blast the Burdett gang into surrender (8). Feathers puts on her scanty saloon-hostess costume (9), provoking Chance into declaring his love for her by forbidding her to appear like that in public.

1

2

3

A brief introduction to *Butch Cassidy and the Sundance Kid* states: 'Not that it matters, but most of what follows is true'. The author was correct on both counts; the film *is* firmly based on the story of two outlaws at the turn of the century and it really does *not* matter that it is true, for it is one thing to base a script on real events and quite another to claim that the results are a 'true' representation of the facts.

The film is largely a vehicle for the Butch Cassidy (Paul Newman) and Sundance Kid (Robert Redford) relationship and the cinema has probably never produced a more endearing pair of villains. Butch is the thinker, a man who has vision 'and the rest of the world wears bifocals'. Sundance is the strong, more traditional type of Western hero who never uses two words when one will do. Together they rob banks and trains with such appealing politeness and ever-present incompetence that it is impossible not to like them.

For both actors it was an important film. Newman's previous major successes had been in roles where he was a rebellious loner – *The Hustler* (1961), *Hud* (1963), *Cool Hand Luke* (1967) – and his attempts at comedy are best forgotten.

6

You never met a pair like Butch and The Kid

They're Taking Trains... They're Taking Banks And They're Taking One Piece Of Baggage!

20th Century-Fox presents

PAUL NEWMAN
ROBERT REDFORD
KATHARINE ROSS

BUTCH CASSIDY AND THE SUNDANCE KID

A George Roy Hill–Paul Monash Production Co-Starring STROTHER MARTIN, JEFF COREY, HENRY JONES
Executive Producer PAUL MONASH Produced by JOHN FOREMAN Directed by GEORGE ROY HILL Written by WILLIAM GOLDMAN
Music Composed and Conducted by BURT BACHARACH A NEWMAN-FOREMAN Presentation PANAVISION® COLOUR BY DE LUXE

Butch and Sundance, having extricated themselves from a card-game dispute (1), return to the Hole-in-the-Wall Gang's hideout (2) where Butch finds his leadership challenged by Harvey Logan (3). He re-establishes command but nevertheless accepts Harvey's idea of holding up the Union Pacific Flyer on successive runs.

After the first hold-up Sundance seeks out the attentions of teacher Etta Place and Butch demonstrates the wonders of a bicycle to the tune of 'Raindrops Keep Fallin' on My Head' (4).

The second Flyer hold-up is less accomplished than its predecessor; too much dynamite is used on the safe, and as the gang collects the scattered bank

notes (5) another train appears. It contains a Superposse which had been formed with the specific purpose of eliminating the menace of Butch and Sundance.

Several members of the gang are shot down, but Butch and Sundance escape. However, the pursuit is relentless (6) and they become faced with the choice between a hopeless shoot-out or

7

8

4

5

Yet his screen relationship with Redford belied what had gone before; he gave a relaxed, amiable performance with a faintly sarcastic humour failing to mask a genuine affection for his partner.

But if the film was a well-received step in a new direction for Newman, it was a major milestone for Redford. *The Sundance Kid* quite simply made him one of the cinema's great names. The role drew attention to his good looks and even though the script offered him few words, the lines were good enough for him to prove that he was a competent actor.

Although the stars' performances were universally acclaimed and gave the film its identity, the Oscars went elsewhere: to William Goldman for his screenplay, Conrad Hall for cinematography, and Burt Bacharach for his musical score and – with lyricist Hal David – best song, 'Raindrops Keep Fallin' on My Head'. There were nominations for Best Picture and Best Direction but the film lost out to John Schlesinger's *Midnight Cowboy* (1969) in both instances.

However, the awards it received

were a reflection that the film sought to entertain – it looked and sounded good. The ideas were not always startlingly original, with several echoing Arthur Penn's *Bonnie and Clyde* released two years earlier, but they were executed with style. For example, the sepia shots that open the film, depict the New York sojourn of Butch, Sundance and Etta (Katharine Ross), and provide the final image of the shoot-out, are strikingly effective. The middle sequence makes use of over three hundred stills in the space of a few minutes, an exciting piece of cinema that deserved to work.

It is ironic that William Goldman won his award for a screenplay which had an economy of words bordering on the miserly, but he relied on a terse, witty repartee between the two outlaws to create a feeling of jaunty optimism, combined with occasional moments of perceptive seriousness which hint at the inevitability of the final slaughter. 'Dammit, why is everything we're good at illegal?' they ask. 'Who are those guys?' they wonder in desperation as the law, in the shape of the Superposse, tries to catch up with them.

Their conversation has a casual, wry humour which at times is so

anachronistic as to be absurd, but which works nevertheless. During the chase Butch asks Sundance 'I think we lost 'em. Do you think we lost 'em?' and when the reply is 'no' continues 'Neither do I'.

The lively banter carries on to the end when, surrounded by what looks like the greater part of the Bolivian army, they debate the possibility of emigrating to Australia. By then the opposition has mounted to impossible odds and their words have a pathos which the humour cannot hide.

Goldman has been taken to task for the lack of realism in his script and his interpretation of the story, for there is a great deal of evidence to suggest that Butch Cassidy survived and returned to the United States where he opened a business making adding machines.

However, the film that represents the West as it really was has probably yet to be made, as the cult of the Western has long since eclipsed the reality of its subject matter. The cinema presents a stylized, often romantic view of an era that provided – as with *Butch Cassidy and the Sundance Kid* – rich story pickings which could be embellished and transformed into entertainment. JOHN THOMPSON

Directed by George Roy Hill, 1969

prod co: Campanile Productions/20th Century-Fox. A Newman-Foreman presentation. **prod:** John Foreman. **sc:** William Goldman. **photo** (Panavision, De Luxe Colour): Conrad Hall. **ed:** John C. Howard, Richard C. Meyer. **art dir:** Walter M. Scott, Chester L. Bayhi. **mus:** Burt Bacharach. **song:** 'Raindrops Keep Fallin' on My Head' by Burt Bacharach, Hal David, sung by B. J. Thomas. **r/t:** 110 minutes.

Cast: Paul Newman (*Butch Cassidy*), Robert Redford (*The Sundance Kid*), Katharine Ross (*Etta Place*), Strother Martin (*Percy Garris*), Henry Jones (*bicycle salesman*), Jeff Corey (*Sheriff Bledsoe*), George Furth (*Woodcock*), Cloris Leachman (*Agnes*), Ted Cassidy (*Harvey Logan*), Kenneth Mars (*marshal*), Donnelly Rodes (*Mason*), Jody Gilbert (*fat lady*), Timothy Scott ('*News' Carver*), Don Keefer (*fireman*), Charles Dierkop ('*Flat Nose' Curry*), Francisco Cordova (*bank manager*), Nelson Olmstead (*photographer*), Paul Bryar, Sam Elliott (*card players*), Charles Akins (*bank employee*), Eric Sinclair (*Tiffany salesman*), Dave Dunlap (*member of the gang*), Percy Helton (*old man*).

...near-suicidal leap from a clifftop. They leap (7).
Worried by their growing notoriety and the posse's professionalism, Butch, Sundance and Etta head for South America after a short stay in New York. Bolivia's banks are the new target, but life again becomes dangerous as their reputation spreads from town to town.

Etta decides to return to the United States (9), leaving Butch and her lover to 'go straight' as payroll guards. However, they are robbed, and after retrieving the money return to outlaw status. While eating at an inn they are recognized and a detachment of the Bolivian army surrounds the town. Escape is finally made impossible (10).

10

THE WILD BUNCH

The Wild Bunch is bracketed by two extraordinary set-pieces of chaotically lethal action. The film begins with the frantic shoot-up – slaughtering sundry innocent bystanders – that ensues from the Bishop gang's aborted raid on the Starbuck bank; and ends with the orgiastic ritual of destruction in which – hugely outnumbered – the gang's ultimate survivors go down fighting as they manage to take a horde of Mapache's troops to perdition with them. Never before had carnage been so graphically or operatically wrought upon the screen.

It is probably these that are the sequences which pin down the film in the popular memory. For all that its protagonists – ageing gunfighters stranded by the rising tide of modern life – are men out of their time, Peckinpah's movie coincided spectacularly (in all senses) with a given moment in film history. Although Arthur Penn's *Bonnie and Clyde* (1967) two years earlier had pointed the way to a treatment of death and injury both franker and more elaborate than had previously been deemed acceptable, it was

The Wild Bunch that fully embraced this development. 'I wanted to show,' said Peckinpah, 'what the hell it feels like to get shot.'

In some of Peckinpah's subsequent films his preoccupation with savagery may become sterile or even absurd, and the slow-motion effects which – following Penn's example – he put to such striking use in *The Wild Bunch* would later, in his own and other hands, become a cliché. But here the explicitness of the scenes of carnage completely unites with the implications of the material: the members of the Wild Bunch can only achieve a kind of meaning for themselves in obliteration by violent death.

At one level, of course, the movie offers a repudiation of the chivalric trappings of the Western genre: Peckinpah extends the conventions of the anti-Westerns of a decade earlier, such as Delmer Daves' *Cowboy* (1958). Unlike the hired guns of *The Magnificent Seven* (1960), Bishop and his followers do not sign up on the side of the oppressed Mexican peasantry, but

rather with their corrupt oppressors. Indeed, the desperadoes who comprise the Bunch, ready to shoot down perfunctorily one of their own wounded when he is unable to keep up with them, would surely in an earlier vintage have been treated as antagonists rather than the 'heroes'.

Finally, though, and not simply through the force of Lucien Ballard's magisterial wide-screen images of horsemen traversing daunting landscapes and engaging in exploits of derring-do (such as the dynamite nonchalantly touched-off with a lighted cigar in the train robbery), the vision which the film asserts is a romantic one. The plot crucially turns on the mutual dependence of Bishop and Thornton (played with marvellously haggard strength by Robert Ryan), and the former clearly accepts that Thornton's dilemma in becoming the 'Judas goat' of the railroad bosses stems from Bishop's own

earlier lapse in allowing his old comrade to be captured.

There is, too, an almost luxuriant romanticism about the Mexican villagers' ceremonial farewell to Bishop and his men, a sequence which is repeated by Peckinpah at the film's very end. And eventually – though too late – the Bunch themselves set aside their façade of cynical pragmatism in abandoning Angel to his fate, and commit themselves to an heroically suicidal gesture on his behalf: 'This time,' declares Pike Bishop, 'let's do it right'.

The Wild Bunch is not without flaws: there is too apparent a recourse to literary metaphor in the deployment of children for ironic effect, and in such details as the vultures which symbolize the degenerate bounty hunters. But the defects fade to unimportance within the grandeur of the overall design. This is a movie of true size.

TIM PULLEINE

Directed by Sam Peckinpah, 1969
Prod co: Warner Brothers/Seven Arts. **prod:** Phil Feldman. **assoc. prod:** Roy N. Sickner. **prod man:** William Faralla. **2nd unit dir:** Buzz Henry. **sc:** Walon Green, Sam Peckinpah, from a story by Walon Green, Roy N. Sickner. **photo** (Technicolor, Panavision 70): Lucien Ballard. **ed:** Louis Lombardo. **art dir:** Edward Carrere. **mus:** Jerry Fielding. **sd:** Robert J. Miller. **ass dir:** Cliff Coleman, Fred Gamon. **r/t:** 145 minutes.
Cast: William Holden (*Pike Bishop*), Ernest Borgnine (*Dutch*), Robert Ryan (*Deke Thornton*), Edmond O'Brien (*Sykes*), Warren Oates (*Lyle Gorch*), Jaime Sanchez (*Angel*), Ben Johnson (*Hector Gorch*), Emilio Fernandez (*Mapache*), Strother Martin (*Coffer*), L. Q. Jones (*T. C.*), Albert Dekker (*Harrigan*), Bo Hopkins (*Crazy Lee*), Bud Taylor (*Wainscoat*), Jorge Russek (*Zamorra*), Alfonso Arau (*Herrera*), Chano Urueta (*Don José*), Sonia Amelio (*Teresa*), Aurora Clavel (*Aurora*), Elsa Cardenas (*Elsa*).

The place is Texas, the year 1914. Disguised as soldiers, the Wild Bunch – an outlaw gang led by Pike Bishop and his sidekick Dutch – ride into Starbuck to rob the bank of a railroad payroll (1). But an ambush has been prepared by the rail bosses, who have had Pike's former comrade Deke Thornton released from a prison sentence to lead a band of bounty hunters against the Bunch (2).

The ambush goes wrong, and in a hail of crossfire many of the townspeople are killed. Most of the gang escape, and after picking up their veteran comrade Sykes, deemed too old for action, they head into Mexico. There they encounter the villainous warlord 'General' Mapache (3), who hires them to steal guns from an American army munitions train. When Angel, a patriotic Mexican who rides with the Bunch, finds his girl is living with Mapache, a bloodbath is narrowly averted (4). After resting-up at Angel's home village, the gang goes ahead with the train robbery (5).

Bishop realizes that Thornton will be onto the scheme, but succeeds in outwitting him. Once the train has been held up, Mapache attempts to double-cross the Bunch in a canyon (6), but he is forestalled and has to pay up. However, Mapache finds out that Angel has given some of the stolen guns to Mexican revolutionaries, and takes him prisoner (7).

Initially, the Bunch abandon Angel to his fate, but after seeing him tortured by Mapache, Pike, Dutch and the Gorch brothers (Sykes is left behind as look-out) enter Mapache's camp and demand Angel's release. In reply Mapache slits Angel's throat (8); Pike shoots Mapache dead (9), precipitating a bloody pitched battle between the Bunch and Mapache's troops, ending with no survivors (10). Later, Sykes appears on the scene with a group of revolutionaries; Thornton also arrives and decides to join them.

81

They'd never forget the day he drifted into town.

CLINT EASTWOOD
HIGH PLAINS DRIFTER

CO-STARRING
VERNA BLOOM
MARIANA HILL
MUSIC BY
DEE BARTON
WRITTEN BY
ERNEST TIDYMAN
DIRECTED BY
CLINT EASTWOOD
PRODUCED BY
ROBERT DALEY
EXECUTIVE PRODUCER
JENNINGS LANG
A UNIVERSAL/
MALPASO CO. PRODUCTION
TECHNICOLOR®
PANAVISION®

A Universal Picture
Distributed by
Cinema International Corporation

Cert. X

Pizza (or Pasta) Westerns

A new title for a famous movie menu. And the main ingredients? Clint Eastwood, a phantom of the plains swathed in the folds of his poncho; Lee Van Cleef, a grimacing black hawk – Zorro unmasked; a host of grubby villains with bandoliers over their shoulders; and the vision of director Sergio Leone, his cameras focused relentlessly on an echoing wasteland of blood and sand

The 'spaghetti' Western was never an accurate label. Spaghetti is all very well, a wholesome base for sauces, meats, clams, garlic and butter. But spaghetti is bland and monotonous to the eye, and the movies that bore the name were always startling visual events. The 'pizza' Western would have been closer, if you can imagine the lurid sunrise of bubbling cheese, the terracotta menace of pepperoni and the inevitable blood-bath of tomato paste. Pizzas are a sight to behold – if only they made them in CinemaScope shapes, they would be the perfect culinary equivalent for Sergio Leone's hallucinatory films. Except that most of them were actually shot in Spain. Perhaps the example really needed is paella – a desert background of saffron with the violent splashes of pimento, shrimp and chorizo.

These *are* edible films; they have so much ham in them. They are filled with stylized violence and cruelty; they are as serpentine with intrigue as they are loyal to the idea of destiny as the far, flat horizon. They know no other human impulses than greed, treachery, silent honour and the unswerving imperative of revenge, but they cannot be taken seriously. The Westerns made by Sergio Leone and Clint Eastwood are deliberate parodies, or fakes. They mark the end of the trustworthiness of the genre and the onset of a new riot of campness. It is as if the Western, and the American history it seems to represent, had been handed over to a director of television commercials for cheroots, serapes and hard liquor. The significance of the 'spaghetti' Western is not just that non-Americans took over the genre, but that American audiences could no longer believe in their own greatest legend.

Early appetizers

There were uncompromising Westerns made in America in the Fifties, pictures that believed in the frontier, in the sheriff's essential role and in the epic dimension of heroism and landscape. *High Noon* (1952), *Shane* (1953) and the films of Anthony Mann are filled with genuine respect for physical space, small communities and a man's moral decision. But by the end of the decade, the Western was less convinced and far less solemn. Howard Hawks' *Rio Bravo* (1959) is a self-conscious reappraisal of the situation in *High Noon*, but it is also a game in which actors in cowboy hats and Western settings exchange the lines of a modern comedy. For Hawks, both *Red River* (1948) and *The Big Sky* (1952) had believed in the nineteenth century, in real space and problems to be overcome. *Rio Bravo* is a largely interior film in which the archetypal figures of John Wayne and Walter Brennan meet the unmistakably up-to-date Dean Martin, Ricky Nelson and Angie Dickinson. There are moments when the old situations are played straight, but *Rio Bravo*'s inner elegance and wit come from the sense of a stale ritual being jazzed up for 1959. Around the same time, old-timers like George Marshall and Raoul Walsh directed deflating comic Westerns, *The Sheepman* and *The Sheriff of Fractured Jaw* (both 1958). Newcomer Arthur Penn took the Billy the Kid saga, in *The*

Left-Handed Gun (1958), and gave it levels of psychological insight that would have terrified Robert Taylor, who played the outlaw in the 1941 version of *Billy the Kid*.

This is all relevant to the 'spaghetti' Western, for the parody could not occur before the myth of the West had been questioned. By 1960, with John F. Kennedy's manner suggesting the ultimate sheriff could be more like Cary Grant than John Wayne, America was suspicious of its own reliance on Western ethics as a basis for foreign policy. The new, ashamed awareness of Native Americans – so recently 'redskins' or 'hostiles' – was prompting a fresh study of frontier history. With *The Man Who Shot Liberty Valance* (1962) and *Cheyenne Autumn* (1964), even John Ford offered a sketchy apology for the wholesale dishonesty with which Hollywood had gilded the West. But on television, night after night, the same

lies were still being perpetrated in series like *Gunsmoke*, *Wells Fargo*, *Wagon Train* and *Rawhide*. Perhaps that was the final excess that made the Western seem sour and laid it open for satire.

Clint in the sun

Clint Eastwood was a veteran of *Rawhide*, but less than a star, when he went to Europe in 1964 to make *Per un Pugno di Dollari* (*A Fistful of Dollars*), a German-Spanish-Italian co-production, directed by Sergio Leone and shot in southern Spain. The headquarters of the Italian film industry, Cinecittà, had already tried to copy several American genres. But nothing matched the success of *A Fistful of Dollars*, a

83

Above, from left to right: icons of the 'spaghetti Western – the good (Clint Eastwood), the bad (Lee Van Cleef), the ugly (Eli Wallach), the vicious (Gian Maria Volonté), the demonic (Henry Fonda) and the bounty – a sackful of dollars. Left: Claudia Cardinale as chief mourner Jill McBain in Once Upon a Time in the West; *she has arrived in Flagstone to join her husband and family at their ranch, only to find them all brutally slaughtered by a vicious outlaw gang trying to force the sale of their land to the railroad*

rewrite the bad scripts and, since he and Leone had no language in common, Eastwood cut out a lot of his dialogue to avoid directing problems. His character, the Man With No Name, became a beautiful but nearly absurd icon of taciturnity. He was an angel of death squinting into the sun, given weird grace by the serape, the cheroot and the wide-brimmed hat, and always glorified in Leone's audacious but equally mannered use of TechniScope.

Second and third courses

A Fistful of Dollars was so successful that it launched a trilogy. But whereas the first picture had been 96 minutes long, the others, *Per Qualche Dollari in Più* (1966, *For a Few Dollars More*) and *Il Buono, il Brutto, il Cattivo* (1967, *The Good, the Bad and the Ugly*), were 130 and 161 minutes. Leone slowed the pace, turning tension into a mocking treacle. The music of Ennio Morricone – like a rattlesnake in a drum-kit – added to the tongue-in-cheek menace. There was always a strong supporting cast: Gian Maria Volonté, in the first two; Lee Van Cleef in the last two. Van Cleef had been one of the gunmen in *High Noon*; Eli Wallach, who is in *The Good, the Bad and the Ugly*, had been the bandit chief in *The Magnificent Seven*.

Eastwood was established, and he would become one of the most commercially reliable stars of the Seventies as well as an adventurous director-producer. *Hang 'Em High* (1968), in which he starred soon after his return to America, is a spaghetti dish in the Hollywood style. Indeed it could be argued that the laconic, vengeful and supreme Harry Callahan, the cop Eastwood plays in *Dirty Harry* (1971) and its sequels, is cousin to the Man With No Name. In 1973 Eastwood directed and starred in *High Plains Drifter*, an absurdist Western that must have made Leone proud.

Leone himself made two more notable pictures. *C'Era una Volta il West* (1968, *Once Upon a Time in the West*) is his best film – his most extreme, formal and ridiculous arrangement of Western imagery, a feast of colour, space and

phenomenon that seems to spring from the sardonic visual imagination of Leone and the hitherto unappreciated smouldering glamour in Eastwood's screen presence.

The film was a rip-off from the Akira Kurosawa film, *Yojimbo* (1961). But that was reasonable, for Kurosawa had often owned up to the way his seemingly authentic samurai films had been inspired by Westerns. Truly, the Western had become a kind of Esperanto; no wonder no-one trusted it. In 1960 John Sturges had made *The Magnificent Seven* as a tribute to Kurosawa's *Shichinin No Samurai* (1954, *Seven*

Samurai). The spectacular violence of that 'remake' and its Mexican settings influenced the films of Sam Peckinpah as well as the Italian Westerns. The seven, though, had been noblemen ready to die for their cause; Leone's invention was to make sleaziness and dishonesty the new norms. His pictures are full of unwashed, unshaved bandidos, the refugees from horror pictures. You know that they can't be trusted because their lip movements never fit what they are saying.

There was reason enough for Eastwood to say nothing. The actor was encouraged to

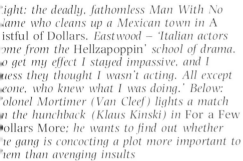

Right: the deadly, fathomless Man With No Name who cleans up a Mexican town in A Fistful of Dollars. *Eastwood – 'Italian actors come from the Hellzapoppin' school of drama. To get my effect I stayed impassive, and I guess they thought I wasn't acting. All except Leone, who knew what I was doing.' Below: Colonel Mortimer (Van Cleef) lights a match on the hunchback (Klaus Kinski) in* For a Few Dollars More; *he wants to find out whether the gang is concocting a plot more important to them than avenging insults*

Jacobean ritual. There is no Eastwood in it, but the film has Henry Fonda as a deliciously wicked lead, along with Jason Robards Jr, Charles Bronson, Jack Elam, Woody Strode, Keenan Wynn and Claudia Cardinale, who has to take the leering abuse that is obligatory for voluptuous women in these films. *Giù la testa* (1972, *A Fistful of Dynamite*) is remarkable for two ham-size performances: Rod Steiger as a Mexican outlaw; James Coburn as an IRA revolutionary.

The 'spaghetti' Western is not common now. Leone's films are few and far between, and Eastwood has moved further towards comedy. But its influence is total. There are so few Westerns made today because the genre has been revealed as not a true fable of rock, lead and dust, but a fabrication of pasta.

DAVID THOMSON

LITTLE BIG MAN

WAS EITHER THE MOST NEGLECTED HERO IN HISTORY OR A LIAR OF INSANE PROPORTION!

DUSTIN HOFFMAN
"LITTLE BIG MAN"
A Cinema Center Films Presentation

MARTIN BALSAM · JEFF COREY · CHIEF DAN GEORGE

Screenplay by Calder Willingham
Based on the Novel by Thomas Berger

FAYE DUNAWAY
AS MRS PENDRAKE

A National General Pictures Release
Panavision® Technicolor® **GP**

Produced by Stuart Millar · Directed by Arthur Penn

Directed by Arthur Penn, 1970

Prod co: Stockbridge/Hiller. A Cinema Center Films Presentation. **prod:** Stuart Millar. **assoc. prod:** Gene Lasko. **sc:** Calder Willingham, from the novel by Thomas Berger. **photo** (Technicolor, Panavision): Harry Stradling Jr. **ed:** Dede Allen. **art dir:** Anglo Graham. **cost:** Dorothy Jeakins. **mus:** John Hammond. **add mus:** John Strauss. **sd:** Al Overton Jr. **sd eff:** James A. Richard, Frank E. Warner. **ass dir:** Mike Moder. **prod man:** Dick Gallegly. **r/t:** 139 minutes.

Cast: Dustin Hoffman (*Jack Crabb*), Faye Dunaway (*Mrs Pendrake*), Martin Balsam (*Allardyce T. Merriweather*), Richard Mulligan (*General George A. Custer*), Chief Dan George (*Old Lodge Skins*), Jeff Corey (*Wild Bill Hickok*), Amy Eccles (*Sunshine*), Kelly Jean Peters (*Olga*), Carole Androsky (*Caroline*), Robert Little Star (*Little Horse*), Cal Bellini (*Younger Bear*), Ruben Moreno (*Shadow That Comes In Sight*), Steve Shemayne (*Burns Red In the Sky*), William Hickey (*historian*), James Anderson (*sergeant*), Jesse Vint (*lieutenant*), Alan Oppenheimer (*major*), Thayer David (*Reverend Silas Pendrake*), Philip Kenneally (*Mr Kane*), Jack Bannon (*captain*), Ray Dimas (*young Jack Crabb*), Alan Howard (*adolescent Jack Crabb*), Jack Mullaney (*card player*), Steve Miranda (*Younger Bear as a youth*), Lou Cutell (*Deacon*), M. Emmet Walsh (*shotgun guard*), Emily Cho (*Digging Bear*), Cecilia Kootenay (*Little Elk*), Linda Dyer (*Corn Woman*), Dessie Bad Bear (*Buffalo Wallow Woman*), Len George (*Crow Scout*), Norman Nathan (*Pawnee*), Helen Verbit (*madame*), Bert Conway (*bartender*), Earl Rosell (*trooper*), Ken Mayer (*sergeant*), Bud Cokes (*man at bar*), Rory O'Brien (*assassin*), Tracy Hotchner (*flirtatious girl*).

Halfway through *Little Big Man* Jack Crabb's comic, meandering adventures explode into tragedy with the massacre of the Cheyenne Indians who have adopted him. Jack watches helplessly as Custer's cavalrymen cut down his young family.

He is a fictitious hero, but many of the scenes he witnesses are based on truth. The unsolicited carnage that took place on the banks of the Washita River in November 1868 was part of General Sheridan's campaign to beat the Cheyenne into submission, or seemingly to exterminate the tribe completely. Ralph Nelson's *Soldier Blue* was released a week before *Little Big Man* and showed the horrors of the 1864 Sand Creek massacre when cavalrymen annihilated over 130 members – mostly women and children – of the same peaceful Cheyenne faction who were supposedly under army *protection*.

So, was Hollywood suddenly, in 1970, atoning for its history of collaboration in white America's unbridled imperialist savagery towards the red man? Or did Penn and Nelson's films sardonically echo the 1968 events at My Lai in Vietnam, thereby suggesting that nothing ever changes?

Whatever the reasons, *Little Big Man*, a film criticized for the structural anomaly that allows the Washita tragedy to merely interrupt the comedy, and *Soldier Blue*, ravaged for its apparently gratuitous violence, at least attempted to redress the historical imbalance perpetrated by Hollywood since Westerns were first made.

In many ways *Little Big Man* should have been the last Western: it embodies and destroys the old heroic myths that had always been the genre's stock-in-trade. With the distancing device of an 121-year-old narrator living out his last days in modern America and with the caustic vision of a film-maker saying goodbye not just to the past but to nostalgia itself, Penn ridicules the legendary conceptions of such figures as the gunfighter (portrayed as an absurd, squinting dude by Dustin Hoffman) and in particular of Wild Bill Hickok (shot ingloriously in the back, as indeed he was in reality). Also under fire are the traditional Western figures of the cure-all medicine salesman-

86

Jack Crabb, 121-year-old survivor of the Indian wars, tells his life story to a historian (1).

As a boy, Jack and his sister Caroline are orphaned by the Pawnees and brought up by Chief Old Lodge Skins of the Cheyenne. Jack's bravery during an attack on the Pawnees earns him the name Little Big Man, but an encounter with the cavalry (2) leads to his return to white civilization.

His education is continued by the Reverend Pendrake and his amorous wife (3), and later by the quack doctor Allardyce T. Merriweather (4), but it is Caroline who introduces him to firearms. Jack becomes a gunfighter, befriends Wild Bill Hickok (5) and marries Olga, a Swedish immigrant who is captured by Indians. Jack joins Custer's cavalry to find her but deserts during an attack on the Cheyenne. While on the run he discovers Sunshine, a squaw who has just given birth to a baby (6). They return to Old Lodge Skins' camp and Sunshine becomes Jack's new wife. However, his happiness is cut short when Custer attacks. Jack rescues the old chief but Sunshine and her child are slaughtered with the rest of the Cheyenne.

After failing to kill Custer, Jack becomes an alcoholic (7) and opts for the life of a hermit. However, he allows himself to be hired as a scout by Custer.

Completely insane, Custer makes his last stand at the Little Big Horn (8). Jack is saved by the warrior Younger Bear and rejoins Old Lodge Skins. Together they go to the resting place of the Cheyenne where the chief prepares to die. His time has not yet come, however, and he and Jack return to the camp (9).

Jack's story over, his interviewer leaves him.

showman (Allardyce T. Merriweather literally loses a limb for each new act of chicanery) and the pure, fresh-faced frontierswoman (the preacher's wife ends up in a brothel). The romantic, Fordian notion of the horse soldiers, all martial grace as they advance majestically through the snow to the tune of 'Garry Owen', pennants flying, is sustained with considerable visual beauty by Penn. However, the same cavalrymen suddenly become indiscriminate butchers; Custer meanwhile is portrayed as a preening, murderous braggart and paranoiac.

It is for the Indians – 'the Human Beings' – that Penn reserves his affection and esteem. They are shown as a wise, brave, spiritually harmonious people who are safe from the hypocrisies that taint the white men in the film: Jack's squaw, unhindered by the false Christian morality of whites, is eager that her widowed sisters (equally eager) should share her husband's body with her. In a reversal of that situation the Reverend Pendrake casts out his unfaithful wife. But, encountering her later in a brothel, Jack recognizes her tawdriness and without bothering to sleep with her he leaves a pile of gold nestling on her naked midriff.

However, Penn never implies that the Cheyenne are perfect. They too have their misfits – but they tolerate them. Indian society has a place for both the effeminate Little Horse who, unable to stand a 'man's' life, stays at home with the squaws, and for the contrary Younger Bear, an angry youth who rebels by washing in the dust, says goodbye when he should say hello, paints himself in evil zigzags and eventually becomes the ferocious warrior who prevails at the Battle of the Little Big Horn.

The spiritual centre of the film is Old Lodge Skins, Jack's adoptive grandfather and a Cheyenne visionary and sage. At the tragicomic ending of Little Big Man the old chief, having had a premonition of his own death and knowing that the age of the Cheyenne is over, solemnly lies down on his bier, expecting the spirits to take him. But they don't. Raindrops, like big tears, sting his eyelids as he waits there, unable to shake off life. 'Sometimes the magic works, sometimes it doesn't,' he muses, and he and Jack wander back to his tepee. It is the final ironic twist in the film – the demythification of even the Cheyenne culture.

The Cheyenne are, at the end, no more than a memory in the mind of the ancient Jack Crabb, left alone in an old people's home to reflect sadly on what the white man has done.

GRAHAM FULLER

Country & Westerns

The twanging of banjos or the thunder of gunshots enlivened the soundtracks of films about the rural South and West – country-music movies and Westerns

Above: Stacy Keach as Doc Holliday in Doc *(1971)*

The Seventies began with the greatest of all Western stars, John Wayne, receiving a long-waited Oscar in April 1970 for his performance in Henry Hathaway's *True Grit* (1969). It ended with his death in June 1979.

The years in between can be regarded as the period in which the Western was dragged kicking and screaming into the twentieth century. The genre's characteristic tone of affirmation or elegy, expressing a nineteenth-century confidence about the future, was transformed into a new tone of cynicism and despair, born of a distinctly modern feeling of helplessness and unease. When the USA bicentenary came along in 1976, the Western – the form which, above all, celebrates the triumphant emergence and civilization of America – could not rise to the occasion. The most typical responses came from Robert Altman, with *Buffalo Bill and the Indians . . . or Sitting Bull's History Lesson*, and Arthur Penn, who directed *The Missouri Breaks*. The former shows one of the country's national heroes played by Paul Newman) as a slow-witted and self-deluding clown; the latter presents as its embodiment of law and order a fat, transvestite sadist (an extraordinary creation by Marlon Brando), who specializes in killing from a distance.

It is perhaps not surprising that the Western should go into a phase of irony and self-criticism. John Ford, the doyen of Western directors and the one who had celebrated the pioneering spirit on film in its purest form, had died in 1973. Other great veteran directors of the genre were to die within the following few years – Howard Hawks in 1977, Raoul Walsh in 1980. After *El Dorado* (1967),

Hawks did manage one more variation on his classic *Rio Bravo* (1959), this time called *Rio Lobo* (1970). Significantly, it is one of his darkest films, evoking a world where chivalry between hero and antagonist no longer exists and which seems to be discovering pleasure and sophistication in sadism.

Even Sam Peckinpah was quiet. It seemed the harrowing vision he had presented in *The Wild Bunch* (1969), a film whose nightmarish violence was to reverberate influentially through other directors' Westerns, had exhausted his sensibilities. His major contribution was the distinguished *Pat Garrett and Billy the Kid* (1973), a study of cynical pragmatism and of adjustment to encroaching civilization. Garrett's pursuit of the Kid takes on an obsessive air as if, by destroying him, he can eradicate his own dubious past.

The death or conversion of the gunfighter so that civilization might prosper is a common theme in Sixties Westerns, expressed most poignantly in Ford's *The Man Who Shot Liberty Valance* (1962). There were numerous Westerns at this time about men whose prowess with a gun has helped to tame the country but who, at the point of transition, have to be rejected for their special skill has become both unnecessary and threatening to the new society. It is a theme that recurs in later Westerns, such as Don Siegel's *The Shootist* (1976) and William Wiard's *Tom Horn* (1979), although the inflection tends to be different. The Sixties had accepted this change as painful, but inevitable and necessary. Seventies films seem more bitter. Tom Horn, for example, is framed, tried and condemned for murder by a society that has no further use for him and fears him. Steve McQueen's performance as Horn, in his penultimate film, was masterly.

During the Seventies the Western suffered the fate of all genres – it became self-conscious. The previous decade had been preoccupied with reflections on the West – on the gap between fact and legend – and the Western hero who was becoming older and more tired. But it then became absorbed with itself as a form – how a Western is constituted, what its main elements are and mean, and how they have been relayed to mass audiences. This self-consciousness appears in several forms. There is the broad comic parody of Mel Brooks' *Blazing Saddles* (1974), an irreverent spoof on basic Western situations. Michael Crichton, the writer and director of *Westworld* (1973), blends cowboy and science fiction in an ingenious tale about programmed robots in a mock frontier town who start killing holiday-makers. In particular, the new films allude to screen history, referring not to the myth of the West but to the mythology of the Western film. Thus, *The Shootist*, which stars John Wayne as an ex-gunfighter dying of cancer, opens with a montage of scenes from earlier Wayne films, blurring the distinction between the specific character he is playing and the general screen persona he had built up over his career. The film becomes an elegy for Wayne himself, who invests the part with enormous dignity. Both Clint Eastwood's *High Plains Drifter* (1973) and *The Missouri Breaks* play on the audience's recognition of the classic Western hero of George Stevens' *Shane* (1953), whose knightly behaviour is mocked and demonized by the two mysterious heroes in both these modern films who also ride in from nowhere to save threatened communities but leave chaos in their wake. Shane (Alan Ladd) was a kind of saviour, an inspirer of men; Eastwood's satanic protagonist in *High Plains Drifter* is an embodiment of what men fear in themselves.

The Seventies Western tends to be short of conventional heroes. With the exception of Eastwood, there was no actor really identifiable as a natural Western star. Indeed, one of the major themes is the decline of heroism, the absence of charisma. This is true even of Westerns that have the names of the central characters in their titles, such as Robert Altman's *McCabe and Mrs Miller* (1971) and Richard Lester's *Butch and Sundance – the Early Days* (1979). In both films the heroes have increasing difficulty in making their presence felt to people busying themselves with the growth of community. And both stage superb gunfights, which are striking precisely because so little notice is taken of them: the townsfolk are too preoccupied to pay much attention to such outmoded confrontations.

The more sceptical and ironical attitude to heroism was probably a response to the infection of cynicism derived from the political traumas of the decade. The influence of the Watergate affair can be felt in a Western such as *Posse* (1975), with Kirk Douglas directing and starring in a sharp little tale about a ruthlessly opportunistic marshal with political ambitions and a mastery of the publicity machine, who is eventually abandoned by supporters (the posse of the title) even more unscrupulous than he is. Vietnam is a ghostly and disturbing shadow through a number of films. Ralph Nelson's *Soldier Blue* and Arthur Penn's *Little Big Man* (both 1970) both recreate the massacre of Indian villages by the US Cavalry as an analogue to the My Lai massacre.

Indeed, the Vietnam experience might explain why so many Seventies Westerns are interested in the years immediately following the American Civil War and the difficulties men find adjusting to post-

war society. In *The Outlaw Josey Wales* (1976), Clint Eastwood directed himself as a man whose quest for revenge (after the murder of his family during the war) is ultimately less important than his desire for peace and healing. On the other hand, two remarkable films about the Jesse James and Cole Younger gangs, Philip Kaufman's *The Great Northfield Minnesota Raid* (1972) and Walter Hill's *The Long Riders* (1980), remain abrasive and disillusioned, presenting characters whose war experience makes it hard for them to put down roots, to conform to a new era of materialism.

A number of Seventies Westerns offer interesting variations on modern social themes. Reflecting a contemporary moral malaise, they often draw little distinction between heroes and villains. John Huston's *The Life and Times of Judge Roy Bean* (1972) makes a hero of the hanging judge. In Robert Benton's *Bad Company* (1971) the outlaws are presented as comically endearing even at their most bestial, and the development of the innocent young hero is an inexorable progress towards crime. In the two Westerns he has made for the director Sydney Pollack, *Jeremiah Johnson* (1972) and *The Electric Horseman* (1979), Robert Redford has used the form to proclaim his particular ecological interests, both films employing the majesty of the landscape and the later one, set in the modern day, showing how a resourceful Westerner can outsmart and humiliate big business. William Fraker's *Monte Walsh* (1970) is concerned with the issue of unemployment in the old West, what happens to cowboys when their skills are superseded by technology: some drift into crime; Monte Walsh himself (Lee Marvin) is offered a job as a circus performer. Turning the offer down, he comments: 'I'm not gonna spit on my whole life.'

Nevertheless, this is one of only two outlets for the Seventies Western hero. The Wild West Show – the aestheticizing and anaesthetizing of frontier adventure – is handled with affectionate respect in Clint Eastwood's *Bronco Billy* (1980); but it is treated savagely in *Buffalo Bill and the Indians . . . or Sitting Bull's History Lesson*, which is concerned not with the West as history or legend but as theatre. The film's iconoclastic proposition is that the West does not represent the heart of American adventurism but the origins of American showbiz.

The other outlet is the rodeo, the modern cinema's arena for the activities of those who still have 'Westering' in their blood. The films with this background – including Cliff Robertson's *J.W. Coop* (1971), Stuart Millar's *When the Legends Die* and Sam Peckinpah's *Junior Bonner* (both 1972) – play

Left: the face of the future Western hero? If so, it is a face that unscrews – Yul Brynner as a robot gunslinger in Westworld. *Above left: Kirk Douglas as the self-seeking marshal whose political ambitions are wrecked in* Posse. *Top left: heading for the last round-up – Monte (Lee Marvin, squatting, centre) and Chet (Jack Palance, kneeling to his left), two cowboys whose time has passed in* Monte Walsh. *Top: the sun goes down on rodeo-rider J.W. Coop (Cliff Robertson). Top right: civilization encroaches on the world of* Bronco Billy, *in which the Wild West Showman (Clint Eastwood) briefly turns train-robber. Above right: revenge-seeking orphan Mattie (Kim Darby) enlists the help of Rooster Cogburn (John Wayne) in* True Grit. *Above: the runaway boys (Jeff Bridges and Barry Brown) of* Bad Company

alternately witty and moving games with the concept of the cowboy in modern civilization. The humour comes from the incongruity of detail, such as the modern cowboy's having to transport his horse by truck in *Junior Bonner*; or the cowboy capitalist in *J.W. Coop* arriving at the rodeo in a jet, pausing only to ask a fellow passenger if he will kindly pass on a message to his broker. When J.W. Coop himself attempts to emulate this champ's life-style and become one of the new jet-propelled whiz-kids of the Wild West circuit, he finds that a cow has nibbled away some of his flying machine.

The conventional Western movie was, then, thoroughly revised in the Seventies. Indeed, *Little Big Man* turned the genre inside out for, as the title suggests, the film is all about paradoxes and contraries. American history is seen through the eyes of an Indian (who is actually a white man); the US Cavalry are referred to as 'savages' and the Indians as 'Human Beings'; an Indian scout offers advice which, as he knows it will be, is reversed by General Custer, a judgment that culminates in the Battle of the Little Big Horn – the classic instance of a soldier advancing his men when they should be retreating. Several of the major characters in the film are shot in the back (they are, it is inferred,

facing the wrong way round), and *Little Big Man* generally is a marvellous inversion of all the old legends, even if it does not go so far as to present the Indian culture through authentically Indian eyes.

It was inevitable that the tragedies of recent American history should feed a retrospective doubt into the legends of its pioneering past. The romantic mode of the Western diminished in the Seventies, being replaced by a visual and verbal realism and brutality that was coupled with a moral ambivalence about the place of violence in American society. Latterday Westerns invariably ask how did America get to this present from that past? Such a question informs their presentation of history, and issues of 'goodies and baddies' take second place to themes such as the growth of racism and capitalism, or the origins of legitimized violence in the American psyche. But the romantic Western myth – the eradication of evil by brave, good and active men – still has the power to stir the imagination. Does it enshrine basic truths, or perpetuate dangerous over-simplifications? The development of the genre could become particularly interesting during the presidency of Ronald Reagan, who not only stands for old-fashioned American values but who can also ride a horse.   NEIL SINYARD

Michael Cimino's
HEAVEN'S GATE

KRIS KRISTOFFERSON · MICHAEL CIMINO'S · HEAVEN'S GATE
CHRISTOPHER WALKEN · JOHN HURT · SAM WATERSTON · BRAD DOURIF
ISABELLE HUPPERT · JOSEPH COTTEN · JEFF BRIDGES
DAVID MANSFIELD · VILMOS ZSIGMOND · JOANN CARELLI · MICHAEL CIMINO

1

4

Directed by Michael Cimino, 1980
Prod co: United Artists. **exec prod:** Denis O'Dell, Charles Okun. **prod:** Joann Carelli. **sc:** Michael Cimino. **photo** (Technicolor): Vilmos Zsigmond. **sp eff:** Paul Stewart, Ken Pepiot, Stan Parks, Sam Price, Jim Camomile, Kevin Quimbell, Tom Burman, Tom Hoerber. **ed:** Tom Rolf, William Reynolds, Lisa Fruchtman, Gerald Greenberg. **art dir:** Tambi Larsen, Spencer Deverill, Maurice Fowler. **set dec:** Jim Berkey, Josie MacAvin. **cost:** Allen Highfill. **chor:** Eleanor Fazan. **mus:** David Mansfield, Joann Carelli. **add mus:** 'The Blue Danube' performed by The New York Philharmonic Orchestra conducted by Leonard Bernstein. **sd:** James J. Klinger, Richard W. Adams, Winston Ryder, Darin Knight. **ass dir:** Michael Grillo, Brian Cook. **prod man:** Charles Okun, Bob Grand, Peter Price. **r/t:** 148 mins.
Cast: Kris Kristofferson (*Averill*), Christopher Walken (*Champion*), John Hurt (*Irvine*), Sam Waterston (*Canton*), Brad Dourif (*Mr Eggleston*), Isabelle Huppert (*Ella*), Joseph Cotton (*The Reverend Doctor*), Jeff Bridges (*John H. Bridges*), Roseanne Vela (*beautiful girl*), Ronnie Hawkins (*Wolcott*), Geoffrey Lewis (*trapper*), Nicholas Woodeson (*small man*), Stefan Shcherby (*big man*), Waldemar Kalinowski (*photographer*), Terry Quinn (*Captain Minardi*), John Conley (*Morrison*), Margaret Benczak (*Mrs Eggleston*), James Knobeloch (*Kopestonsky*), Erika Petersen (*Mrs Kopestonsky*), Paul Koslo (*Major Lezak*), Robin Bartlett (*Mrs Lezak*), Tom Noonan (*Jake*), Marat Yusim (*Russian merchant*), Aivars Smits (*Mr Kovach*), Gordana Rashovich (*Mrs Kovach*), Neil Wilson (*Kovach's son*).

Heaven's Gate has become one of the most controversial movies of the last decade, earning comments ranging from 'the event we have been waiting for' to 'an unqualified disaster'. This lavish, epic Western, directed by Michael Cimino, relates the story of the Johnson County Wars – the attempted massacre in Wyoming in 1892 of immigrant small farmers by the wealthy Stock Grower's Association. But the film received such harsh criticism that it was withdrawn from cinemas to be re-edited after only a few days of showing.

The Johnson County War, as the original script was known, was written by Cimino nearly ten years before the film was made. It was only after the enormous financial and critical success of *The Deer Hunter* (1978) – the film that won Cimino an Oscar – that backing was forthcoming. Hollywood was delighted by the new generation of directors and their money-spinning ventures and were prepared to take risks believing it could bring in more profit. United Artists beat Warner Brothers in the race to back Cimino at an initial costing of $7.5 million. Rewriting increased the budget considerably but even the first version of the film cost over $36 million, making it one of the most expensive films ever made.

Cimino is wholeheartedly committed to visual authenticity and spared no costs in re-creating nineteenth-century America. He scoured the country looking for old-fashioned craftsmen. He brought in contemporary firearms and even transported an ancient locomotive miles across country, re-routing it to avoid the smaller, modern railway tunnels. To achieve the large and spectacular crowd scenes, he trained numerous extras to skate, waltz and handle firearms and horses. As a result the look of the film is sumptuous.

United Artists executives began to worry about the escalating costs and Cimino's inability to stick to a shooting schedule. But they believed that the finished product would be worth it and were as unprepared as Cimino for the critical onslaught that the original three-and-a-half hour film received. Pauline Kael wrote in *The New Yorker*:

'I thought it was easy to see what to cut. But when I tried afterward to think of what to *keep* my mind went blank.'

The critics argued that the film's narrative was too complicated to follow, that the extravagant set-pieces were pretentious and the heavy financial outlay purely self-indulgent. The re-edited version (75 minutes shorter) was, however, shown at the Cannes Film Festival and was favourably received by the European press. And it is in Europe that United Artists hope to rescue the film's reputation – and budget.

Finance was not the only problem to beset the production: fighting on the set and an animal lovers' boycott added to the difficulties. Even its factual reliability has been questioned. Some historians have suggested that only two people were killed in the war and that certainly Averill, Champion and Ella played very different roles in real life. Although obsessed with the visual authenticity of a film Cimino is no great stickler for historical accuracy: he defended the Russian-roulette scene in *The Deer Hunter* on the grounds that it was an excellent metaphor for the game of death that war forces men to play. Similarly the events and characters of *Heaven's Gate* represent the process through which a new ruling-class emerged in America after the confusion of the Civil War. The long opening sequence of the Harvard graduation ceremony, the pompous speeches and elaborate newly-found traditions, set the scene, playing an equivalent role to the wedding in *The Deer Hunter*. It locates the action that follows against the aspirations and ideals of America's wealthier families. Averill and Irvine, both representatives of their class, go West. Irvine reluctantly sides with the Association who have the implicit backing of the government but Averill betrays his origins, siding with the immigrant community.

Heaven's Gate is, in the end, a classic Western confrontation between heroes and villains, with the difference that the film is solidly on the side of the poor immigrant farmers. This bias caused the French magazine *Liberation* to call *Heaven's Gate* 'the first socialist Western'.   SALLY HIBBIN

92

James Averill and Billy Irvine, two of the 1870 class of Harvard University (1), join in the dancing, drunkeness and rituals that attend the graduation ceremony.

Twenty years later Averill (2) returns to Casper, Wyoming (3) after a visit East, and is surprised

to find the town crowded with poverty-stricken immigrants looking for work, and is worried to find Association members drawing clothes and arms on the Stock Grower's Association's account. Visiting the Association's club house he meets Irvine, who

reveals the existence of a death-list consisting of the names of 125 small-holders and poor settlers in Johnson County that the wealthy cattle barons want to 'eliminate'.

Back in Sweetwater, the main town of Johnson County where he is the federal lawman, Averill

delivers a birthday present of a pony and trap to Ella (4), the madam of the local brothel, with whom both Averill and Nathan D. Champion, the Association's local hired-gun, are in love.

After a roller-skating birthday party (5) at Heaven's Gate, Sweetwater's community centre, Averill tries to persuade Ella to leave the County for safety. The next day he publicly reveals the names on the death-list, among which Ella's name appears.

Champion asks Ella to marry him and she accepts. Averill accuses Champion of knowing about the death-list but Champion breaks his affiliation with the Association by killing one of the leaders.

The Association's hired gang of killers are converging on Sweetwater. Ella is nearly raped by members of the gang, but although Averill saves her he arrives too late to stop her girls from being brutally murdered. Champion (6) is also killed by Association men.

The citizens of Sweetwater panic and wildly attack the gang (7), killing many of them including Irvine (8). With Averill's help they organize their attack properly. They are winning when the Wyoming National Guard appear and arrest – or rescue – the remnants of the hired gang.

Rhode Island in 1900. Averill recalls his wedding day when the Association got in one last shot – the one that killed his bride, Ella.

Index

Abbott and Costello, 43
Acord, Art, 23
Across the Wide Missouri, 57, 58
Adventures of Buffalo Bill, The, 8
Adventures of Captain Marvel, 23
Adventures of Robin Hood, The, 43
Akins, Claude, 62
Alamo, The, 59, 73
Aldrich, Robert, 57, 59
All That Heaven Allows, 38
Allen, Rex, 24
Allied Artists, 24
Along Came Jones, 41
Altman, Robert, 17, 89, 90
Alton, John, 54
Anderson, Broncho Bolli, 48
Anderson, Gilbert M., 20
Anderson, Judith, 55
Andrews, Dana, 28
Annie Oakley, 17
Apache, 18
Archuletta, Beulah, 18
Arizona, 43
Aronson, Max, 20
Arthur, Jean, 17, 19, 27, 59, 67
Aryan, The, 20
August, Joseph, 15
Autry, Gene, 24, 26, 27, 28, 36

Back to Bataan, 72
Bad Bascomb, 40
Bad Company, 90
Badmen of Missouri, 43
Baggot, King, 15
Baker, Bob, 24
Ballad of Cable Hogue, 68
Ballew, Smith, 24
Bancroft, Anne, 19
Bancroft, George, 35
Bar 20 Rides Again, 26
Barbarian and the Geisha, The, 74
Barry, Don 'Red', 24
Barthelmess, Richard, 25
Battle at Elderbush Gulch, The, 9
Baxter, Anne, 17
Baxter, Warnes, 25
Bedford, Barbara, 15
Beery, Wallace, 40
Belle Starr, 28, 43
Ben-Hur, 9
Bend of the River, 42, 55, 56, 58, 68
Bennett, Joan, 27, 28
Benny, Jack, 44
Benton, Robert, 90
Berenger, Tom, 51
Big Country, The, 59
'Big Five' Western stars, 23
Big Jim McLain, 73
Big Sky, The, 18, 83
Big Sleep, The, 23
Big Trail, The, 12, 24, 25, 26, 28, 73, 75
Billy the Kid, 24, 25, 28, 39, 43, 59, 83
Billy the Kid Returns, 49
Birth of a Nation, The, 16
Blazing Saddles, 90
Blood and Sand, 62
Boetticher, Budd, 17, 41, 57, 58, 62–63

Bogart, Humphrey, 28, 41, 43
Bond, Ward, 30, 58, 68
Boone, Richard, 58, 62
Border Incident, 55
Borgnine, Ernest, 17, 80–81
Boyd, William, 24, 26
Brackett, Leigh, 59
Brand, Max, 28
Branded, 42
Brandon, Henry, 67, 89
Brennan, Walter, 11, 27, 28, 41, 44, 58, 59, 83
   filmography, 11
Bridges, Jeff, 91
Bridges, Lloyd, 45
Brigham Young, 43, 45
Broken Arrow, 42, 55, 57, 58
Bronco Billy, 90, 91
Broncho Billy's Redemption, 30
Bronson, Charles, 36, 67, 68, 85
Brooks, Mel, 90
Brown, Barry, 91
Brown, Harry John, 62
Brown, Johnny Mack, 23, 24, 26
Brown, Karl, 9
Brynner, Yul, 91
Buchanan Rides Alone, 62, 63
Buck Benny Rides Again, 44
Buckner, Robert, 28
Buffalo Bill, 8, 41, 43
Buffalo Bill and the Indians . . . or Sitting Bull's History Lesson, 17, 89, 90
Bullion City, 23
Buntline, Ned, 23
Buoni, il Bruto, il Cattivo, Il (The Good, the Bad, and the Ugly), 68, 84
Burr, Raymond, 54
Butch and Sundance – the Early Days, 51, 90
Butch Cassidy and the Sundance Kid, 51, 78–79

Cagney, James, 28, 41, 43, 58
Cahn, Edward, 26
California, 23, 43
Cameron, Rod, 24
Canadian Pacific, 41
Canuff, Yakima, 23
Captain Blood, 43
Capture, The, 46
Cardinale, Claudia, 19, 84, 85
Carey, Harry, Jr, 8, 9, 23, 31, 58, 66
Carradine, John, 17
Carson, Kit, 43
Carson, 'Sunset', 24
Cattle Drive, 41
Cattle Queen of Montana, 58
C'Era una Volto il West (Once Upon a Time in the West), 40, 68, 84
Chandler, Jeff, 58
Chandler, Lane, 23
Chaplin, Geraldine, 17
Chato's Land, 36, 37
Cheyenne Autumn, 18, 31, 32, 49, 83
Christie, Julie, 19
Churchill, Berton, 35
Churchill, Marguerite, 26, 73

Cimmaron, 19, 26, 57, 59
Cimino, Michael, 92
Cisco Kid movies, 25
Claire, Gertrude, 15
Clift, Montgomery, 19, 42, 45, 74
Coburn, James, 19, 62
Cody, Coloneo William F. (Buffalo Bill), 8, 50
Collins, Monte, 15
Colorado Territory, 46
Columbia studies, 23, 24
Comanche Station, 17, 62, 63
Come and Get It, 11
Conquerors, The, 26, 46
Cooper, Gary, 17, 19, 25, 27, 28, 35, 41, 44, 55, 57, 59, 64
Corrigan, Ray 'Crash', 24
Covered Wagon, The, 7, 8, 10, 12–13, 16, 23, 37, 38, 48, 57
Cowboy and the Squaw, The, 48
Cowboys, The, 72, 75
Crawford, Joan, 19, 57, 58, 68
Crichton, Michael, 90
Crimson Trail, The, 22
Cripple Creek Bar Room, 8
Crisp, Donald, 30
Cruze, James, 9, 10, 12, 16, 23, 48
Cukor, George, 59
Cummings, Robert, 28
Curtiz, Michael, 28
Custer's Last Raid, 9, 21

Dakota, 43
Dalton, Emmett, 7, 50, 51
Darby, Kim, 75, 91
Dark Command, 42, 43
Darnell, Linda, 17
Darwell, Jane, 58
Daves, Delmer, 42, 55, 57, 59
David and Bathsheba, 58
Day, Doris, 17
De Havilland, Olivia, 45
DeMille, Cecil B., 24, 27, 28, 43
de Toth, André, 44
de Wilde, Brandon, 59, 67
Dean, Eddie, 24
Decision at Sundown, 17, 62
Deer Hunter, The, 92
del Rio, Dolores, 18
Demarest, William, 41
Desperate, 54
Destry Rides Again, 18, 21, 28, 42, 58
Devil's Doorway, 39, 54, 55, 58
Devine, Andy, 27, 35, 58
Dickinson, Angie, 19, 59, 83
Dietrich, Marlene, 18, 28, 35, 42, 58, 67
Dirty Harry, 84
Dirty Little Psychopath, 49
Distant Drums, 58
Dix, Richard, 10, 26, 28
Doc, 49
Dodge City, 28, 34, 40, 43
Donlevy, Brian, 27, 28
Donovan's Reef, 33
Douglas, Kirk, 30, 49, 57, 90, 91
Downs, Cathy, 17, 52
Dr Broadway, 54
Dru, Joanne, 19, 29, 31, 45, 74
Drums Along the Mohawk, 33

Duel at Silver Creek, 37, 57
Duel in the Sun, 19, 44, 57
Duncan, Captain T. E., 15
Durango Kid, 4
Duryea, Dan, 58
Duvall, Robert, 51
Dwan, Allan, 30

Earp, Wyatt, 49
Eastwood, Clint, 9, 68, 82, 83–85, 90
El Cid, 56
El Dorado, 89
Elam, Jack, 17, 58, 67, 85
Electric Horseman, The, 90
Elliott, Gordon 'Wild Bill', 24
Ellison, James, 27
Emerson, Hope, 58
Ericson, John, 19
Escape from Fort Bravo, 57
Essanay studios, 20
Evans, Dale, 17
Evans, Hal G., 15

Fairbanks, Douglas, 9
Fall of the Roman Empire, The, 56
Famous Players – Lasky studios, 12
Far Country, The, 11, 42, 55, 59
Farrow, John, 57
Fastest Gun Alive, The, 37
FBO studios, 10
Ferber, Edna, 26
Fighting Caravans, 12
Fighting Kentuckian, The, 73
Fighting Seabees, The, 72
Fighting With Kit Carson, 24
Fistful of Dollars, A, 63, 68, 85
Fistful of Dynamite, A, 83, 85
Flaherty, Robert, 12
Fleming, Rhonda, 17
Fleming, Victor, 25, 46
Flippen, Jay C., 57
Flying Tigers, 72
Flynn, Errol, 28, 40, 43, 45, 50
Fonda, Henry, 17, 28, 29, 30, 31, 37, 40, 42, 43, 46, 52, 57, 58, 84, 85
Fontaine, Joan, 28
For a Few Dollars More, 68, 83, 84, 95
Foran, Dick, 24
Ford, Francis, 9, 21
Ford, Glenn, 58, 59
Ford, John, 8, 9, 10, 12, 18, 21, 23, 28, 29–33, 45, 51, 52–53, 57, 67
   filmography, 32–33
Forde, Victoria, 16
Foreman, Carl, 58
Fort Apache, 30, 32, 40, 42, 45, 73
Fort William, 41
Forty Guns, 19, 58
Fox studios, 9, 12, 23
Fraker, William, 90
Francis, Kay, 27
Fuller, Samuel, 19, 58, 68
Furies, The, 19, 55, 56, 58
Furthman, Jules, 59
Fury, 46

Gable, Clark, 58, 59
Gibson, Hoot, 9, 21, 23
Gish, Lillian, 16, 17
Giù la Testa, 85
Glaum, Louise, 16
Go West, 43, 44
God's Country and the Woman, 27
Godard, Jean-Luc, 56, 75
Gold Mine in the Sky, 36
Gold is Where You Find It, 27
Golden Stallion, The, 17
Goldwyn, Samuel, 11
Gone With the Wind, 18, 27, 44
Good, the Bad, and the Ugly, The, 68, 84
Grapes of Wrath, The, 30, 32
Gray, Coleen, 19
Great Flamarion, The, 54
Great Northfield Minnesota Raid, 51, 90
Great Train Robbery, The, 20, 48
Green Berets, The, 73
Grey, Zane, 10, 23
Griffith, D. W., 9, 16, 23
Griggs, Loyal, 59
Gun Fury, 57
Gunfight at the OK Corral, 17, 49
Gunfighter, The, 40, 57, 58, 60–61, 67
Guns in the Afternoon, 41
Gunsmoke, 83
Guthrie, A. B., 59

Hale, Monte, 24
Hang 'Em High, 84
Hangman's House, 75
Hangmen Also Die! 11
Hannie Caulder, 17, 19
Hardy, Oliver, 73
Hart, William S., 8, 9, 12, 14–15, 16, 20, 50–51, 66, 67
Hathaway, Henry, 89
Hawks, Howard, 19, 30, 45, 57, 59, 89
Haycox, Ernest, 34
Hayden, Sterling, 68
Hayward, Susan, 19
Heart of Texas Ryan, The, 21
Heart of the North, 27
Heaven's Gate, 92–93
Heflin, Van, 58, 59, 67
Hell's Hinges, 9, 20
Heller in Pink Tights, 59
Henry, O., 25
Hepburn, Audrey, 18
Heston, Charlton, 56
Hickman, Darryl, 40
High Noon, 17, 37, 38, 41, 46, 57, 58, 64–65, 83
High Plains Drifter, 9, 36, 37, 68, 82, 84, 90
Hill, Walter, 90
Hoffman, Dustin, 50, 86
Hogan, James, 27
Holden, William, 32, 80–81
Holt, Jack, 10, 23
Holt, Jennifer, 23
Holt, Tim, 23, 24
Homeier, Skip, 62
Hondo, 57
Hopalong Cassidy series, 26
Hope, Bob, 43, 58
Horse Soldiers, The, 30, 32, 72, 74
Hough, Emerson, 9
Houston, George, 24
Houston, Sam, 43
How Green Was My Valley, 30, 32
How the West Was Won, 59
Howard, Leslie, 26
Hughes, Howard, 43, 44
Hunt, Marsha, 55
Hunter, Jeffrey, 30, 58, 67
Huston, John, 18, 26, 90
Huston, Walter, 26, 58
Hutton, Betty, 17

In Old Arizona, 25, 43
Ince, Thomas H., 8, 9, 20

Inceville studios, 20
Indians Are Coming, The, 22, 23
Iron Horse, The, 10, 12, 23, 28, 37, 48, 57

J. W. Coop, 90, 91
Jackass Mail, 40
Jennings, Al, 7, 51
Jeremiah Johnson, 90
Jesse James, 23, 27, 28, 34, 41
Johnny Guitar, 19, 57, 58, 68
Johnson, Ben, 29, 31, 58
Jones, Buck, 9, 21, 22, 23
Jones, Jennifer, 44
Jones, L. Q., 62
Jordan, Dorothy, 67
Judge Priest, 30
Junior Bonner, 68, 90, 91
Just Tony, 21

Kaufman, Philip, 90
Keach, Stacy, 49
Kelly, Grace, 17
Kemp, Howard, 56
Kennedy, Arthur, 67, 68
Kennedy, Burt, 63
Kennedy, Joseph P., 35
Kentucky, 11
King Cowboy, 21
King, Henry, 46, 58, 60–61
King Lear, 56
Kinski, Klaus, 85
Kit Carson, 23, 43
Kramer, Stanley, 58
Kurosawa, Akira, 63, 84

Ladd, Alan, 12, 42, 58, 59, 67, 90
Lady of the Dugout, 51
Lane, Allen 'Rocky', 24
Lang, Fritz, 11, 43, 46, 58, 68
LaRue, Al 'Lash', 24
Lash, The, 25
Lasky, Jesse L., 12, 16
Last Drop of Water, The, 9
Last Frontier, The, 19
Last Hunt, The, 39
Last Hurrah, The, 29
Last Train from Gun Hill, 37
Law and Jake Wade, The, 37
Law and Order, 26
Lawman, 37
Le May, Alan, 18
Lease, Rex, 23
Left-Hnaded Gun, The, 59, 83
Leigh, Janet, 55
Leighton, Lillian, 15
Leone, Sergei, 63, 68, 83–85
Leslie, Joan, 19
Lester, Richard, 90
Life and Times of Judge Roy Bean, The, 90
Little Big Man, 50, 86–87, 90, 91
Littlefield, Lucien, 15
Livingston, Bob, 24
Lloyd, Frank, 27
London, Julie, 19
Lone Star, 59
Lonedale Operator, The, 16
Lonely Are the Brave, 37, 68
Lonesome, 63
Long Riders, The, 90
Long Voyage Home, The, 30, 32
Loren, Sophia, 56, 59
Lusty Men, The, 19

MacLaine, Shirley, 59
Magnificent Seven, The, 59, 84
Main, Marjorie, 40
Man From Laramie, The, 31, 42, 54, 55, 56, 59, 67, 68
Man of Conquest, 28, 43
Man of the West, 19, 41, 54, 55
Man Who Shot Liberty Valance, The, 32, 33, 45, 72, 74, 83, 89
Man Without a Star, 30, 57
Mann, Anthony, 19, 31, 42, 54–56, 57, 58, 68
filmography, 56

Marion, George, 15
Marshall, George, 28, 59, 83
Marshall, Tully, 9, 12
Martin, Dean, 59, 76–77, 83
Marin, Mary, 17
Martin, Strother, 17
Marvin, Lee, 19, 32, 33, 37, 62, 90, 91
Marx Brothers, 43, 44
Massacre, The, 9
Mature, Victor, 19, 51
Maverick Queen, The, 58
Maynard, Ken, 10, 21, 22, 23, 25, 26
McCabe and Mrs Miller, 19, 90
McCambridge, Mercedes, 19, 68
McCoy, Colonel Tim, 10, 21, 22, 23, 25
McCrea, Joel, 11, 27, 28, 39, 41, 45
McDonald, Francis, 67
McDowall, Roddy, 32
McGlynn, Frank, Sr, 27
McClintock! 75
McQueen, Steve, 38, 90
Meek, Donaod, 17, 35
Meyer, Emile, 67
MGM studios, 24, 25
Miljan, John, 27
Millar, Stuart, 90
Miller Brothers, 9
Miracle Rider, The, 21
Missouri Breaks, The, 89, 90
Mitchell, Thomas, 30, 35
Mitchum, Robert, 19, 24, 44, 55
Mix, Tom, 9, 10, 15, 16, 21, 22, 24, 25, 28, 48, 75
Monogram studios, 22
Monte Walsh, 90, 91
Montiel, Sarita, 18
Morricone, Ennio, 84
Morris, Wayne, 24
Mother Machree, 75
Mowbray, Alan, 31
Mr Deeds Goes to Town, 37
Mulligan, Richard, 50
Murnan, F. W., 23
Murphy, Audie, 57
Murphy, Jack, 15
My Darling Clementine, 11, 16–17, 30, 31, 37, 40, 45, 49, 52–53, 57
My Pal the King, 21

Naked Spur, The, 42, 55, 56, 57, 68
Nanook of the North, 12
Neill, Richard R., 15
Nelson, Ralph, 86, 90
Nelson, Ricky, 76–77, 83
Nevada Smith, 38
Newill, James, 24
Newman, Paul, 51, 59, 78, 79, 89
Nichols, George, Jr, 28
Night Passage, 57
Nolan, Lloyd, 27
North of 36, 7, 10
North West Mounted Police, 43
Northwest Passage, 11
O'Brien, George, 9, 10, 23
O'Briend, Margaret, 40
O'Connell, Arthur, 55
Of Mice and Men, 23
O'Hara, Maureen, 41
Oklahoma! 57
Oklahoma Kid, The, 28, 34, 41, 43
Once Upon a Time in the West, 37, 40, 67, 68, 84
Only The Valiant, 40
Out of the Past, 55
Outlaw, The, 19, 43, 44
Outlaw Josey Wales, The, 90
Ox-Bow Incident, The, 37, 40, 43, 46–47

Palance, Jack, 59, 67, 91
Paleface, The, 43
Paramount studios, 9, 15, 21
Pat Garrett and Billy the Kid, 19, 89
Payne, John, 30

Peck, Gregory, 17, 40, 44, 58, 60–61, 67
Peckinpah, Sam, 41, 68, 80–81, 84, 89, 90
Penn, Arthur, 59, 83, 86, 89, 90
Pennick, Jack, 30
Per Qualche Dollari in Piu (For a Few Dollars More), 68, 84
Per in Pugno di Dollari (Fistful of Dollars), 63, 68, 83
Perils of Pauline, The, 48
Perkins, Anthony 57, 58
Perrin, Jack, 23
Phantom Empire, The, 24, 26
Pickford, Mary, 26
Pidgeon, Walter, 30
Plainsman, The, 17, 27, 28, 41, 43
Platt, Louise, 16, 17
Pollack, Sydney, 90
Pollard, Michael, J., 49
Pony Express, The, 10
Porter, Edwin S., 8, 20
Posse, 90
Power, Tyrone, 28
Professionals, The, 19
Proud Ones, The, 58
Pursued, 19, 44, 46, 56

Qualen, John, 30, 32
Quiet Man, The, 32, 75

Ramrod, 44, 45
Ranch Life in the Great Southwest, 9
Rancho Notorious, 18, 37, 58, 67, 68
Randall, Jack, 24
Randall, Stuart, 67
'Ranown cycle', 62–63
Raw Deal, 54, 55
Rawhide, 83
Ray, Allene, 22
Ray, Nicholas, 19, 57, 58, 68
Reagan, Ronald, 28, 91
Red River, 11, 19, 38, 42, 45, 57, 74, 83
Redford, Robert, 51, 78–79, 90
Remington, Frederic, 7, 8
Return of Frank James, The, 40
Ride 'Em Cowboy, 43
Ride lonesome, 41, 62
Ride the High Country, 37, 38, 39, 41, 68
Riders of Death Valley, 21
Riders of Destiny, 75
Riders of the Deadline, 24
Riders of the Purple Sage, 21
Rio Bravo, 11, 19, 30, 59, 76–77, 83, 89
Rio Grande, 30, 45, 58, 73, 74
Rio Lobo, 89
Ritter, Tex, 24
RKO studios, 23
Robards, Jason, Jr, 68, 85
Roberts, Pernell, 62
Robinson, Edward G., 41
Rogers, Roy, 17, 20, 24, 28, 49, 51
Rogers, Will, 30
Rooney, Mickey, 21
Ross, Katharine, 78–79
Rosson, Arthur, 27, 28
Rough Riders series, 22
Run for Cover, 41, 58
Run of the Arrow, 18, 68
Russell, J. Gordon, 15
Russell, Jane, 19, 43, 44
Rust, Richard, 62
Ryan, Robert, 19, 55, 58, 80

Saddle Tramp, 41
San Antonio, 43
Sands of Iwo Jima, The, 73, 74
Santa Fe Trail, 28, 43
Savage, Turner, 15
Scarlet Drop, The, 8
Schell, Maria, 19
Scott, Fred, 24
Scott, Randolph, 17, 27, 36, 39, 41, 43, 44, 57, 62–63

Scouts of the Plains, The, 8
Searchers, The, 18, 29, 30, 31, 32, 42, 58, 59, 67, 70–71, 74
Secrets, 76
Selig company, 9
Selznick, David O., 44, 57
Sergeant York, 11
Seven Men From Now, 18, 62, 63
Seven Samurai, 84
Shadow Ranch, 21
Shane, 19, 37, 42, 57, 58, 59, 67, 90
She Wore a Yellow Ribbon, 16, 29, 30, 31, 32, 42, 45, 57, 73, 74
Sheepman, The, 59, 83
Sheriff of Fractured Jaw, The, 83
Shichinin No Samurai (Seven Samurai), 84
Shootist, The, 75, 89, 90
Siegel, Don, 57, 89
Silva, Henry, 62
'Silver King', 23
Silver Lode, 30
Simpson, Russell, 58
Sjöström, Victor, 16
Soldier Blue, 38, 86, 80
Son of Paleface, 58
Spoilers, The, 44
Squaw Man, The, 9
Stagecoach, 10, 16, 17, 24, 27, 28, 29, 30, 34–35, 37, 42, 48, 75
Stand Up and Fight, 39
Stanwyck, Barbara, 17, 19, 55, 56, 58
Starr, Belle, 43
Starrett, Charles, 24
Steele, Bob, 23
Steiger, Rod, 68, 83
Steiner, Max, 28
Stevens, George, 56, 59, 67, 90
Stewart, James, 11, 18, 28, 31, 32, 33, 42, 49, 54, 56, 57, 58, 67
Stoddard, Ransom, 33
Strange Impersonation, 54

Strode, Woody, 19, 85
Sturges, John, 44, 57, 84
Sullivan, C. Gardner, 15
Sun Shines Bright, The, 30
Support Your Local Sheriff, 11
Sweet, Blanche, 16

T-Men, 54, 55
Tall T, The, 18, 62, 63
'Tarzan', 23
Taylor, Elizabeth, 75
Taylor, Robert, 28, 39, 58, 83
Texans, The, 27, 28
Texas, 43
Texas Rangers, The, 27
Texas Streak, The, 22
They Died With Their Boots On, 40, 43, 44, 50
They Were Expendable, 72–73
Thomson, Fred, 10, 23
Threatt, Elizabeth, 18
Three Bad Men, 10, 27
Three Godfathers, 75
3.10 to Yuma, 58, 59
Thundering Herd, The, 10
Tierney, Gene, 28
Tin Star, The, 40, 57, 58
To Have and Have Not, 11
Toll Gate, The, 20
Tom Horn, 89
Tornado, 29
Torrence, Ernest, 9, 12
Tourneur, Jacques, 55
Tracy, Spencer, 11, 29
Trader Horn, 23
Trevor, Claire, 16, 35, 55, 57, 75
Triangle Film Corporation, 20
'Trigger', 17, 20, 21
Trotti, Lamarr, 46
True Grit, 42, 75, 89, 91
Tumbleweeds, 9, 14–15, 21
Tumbling Tumbleweeds, 24, 26, 27
Twelve O'Clock High, 58
Two Guns and a Badge, 24

Two Rode Together, 31
Tyler, Tom, 23

Unconquered, The, 43
Unforgiven, The, 18
United Artists, 15, 21
Union Pacific, 27, 28, 34, 37, 41, 43
Universal studios, 23, 25

Van Cleef, Lee, 83, 84, 85
Van Fleet, Jo, 17
Vanishing American, The, 10
Vera Cruz, 59
Vidor, King, 19, 24, 25, 27, 30, 44, 57
Violent Men, The, 41, 58
Virginia City, 28, 40, 42
Virginian, The, 7, 9, 25, 41, 46
Volga Boatman, The, 24
Volonté, Gian Maria, 84

Wagon Show, The, 10
Wagon Tracks, 12
Wagon Train, 83
Wagonmaster, 29, 30, 31, 38, 58
Wakely, Jimmy, 24
Wales, Ethel, 16
Wales, Wally, 23
Wallach, Eli, 84
Walsh, Raoul, 12, 19, 24, 25, 26, 40, 44, 46, 56, 57, 75, 83, 89
Wanger, Walter, 35
War Paint, 23
Warlock, 37
Warner Brothers, 24, 43
Way of a Mother, The, 8
Wayne, John, 11, 18, 19, 23, 24, 26, 28, 29, 30, 31, 32, 33, 36, 42, 45, 57, 58, 59, 62, 67, 70–71, 72–75, 76–77, 89, 90, 91
    filmography, 74–75
Wedding Night, The, 11
Welch, Raquel, 17, 19

Wellman, William, 43, 46–47, 58, 59
Wells Fargo, 27, 41, 83
Westbound, 62
Western Union, 37, 41, 43
Westerner, The, 11, 28, 38, 41, 44
Westward the Women, 58, 59
Westworld, 90, 91
When the Daltons Rode, 27, 28, 43
When the Legends Die, 90
White Oak, 8
Wiard, William, 89
Widmark, Richard, 40
Wild Bill Hickok, 20
Wild Bunch, The, 80–81, 89
Wild Horse Mesa, 10
Wild North, The, 57, 58
Willat, Irvin, 7, 10
Wilson, 'Whip', 24
Winchester '73, 37, 42, 54, 55, 56, 58, 68
Wind, The, 16, 17
Wings of Eagles, The, 32
Winners of the Wilderness, 23
Winninger, Charles, 30
Wister, Owen, 7
Woman They Almost Lynched, The, 19
Women characters in Westerns, 16–19
Wood, Natalie, 18, 29, 75
Worden, Hank, 31
Words and Music, 75
Wyler, William, 28, 44, 59
Wynn, Keenan, 85
Wyoming, 40, 43

Yellow Sky, 17, 40, 46
Yojimbo, 63, 84
Young Mr Silver, 29, 30

Zanuck, Darryl F., 46, 58
Zinneman, Fred, 46, 57, 58
Zukor, Adolph, 12

Acknowledgments

Many of the illustrations come from stills issued to publicise films made or distributed by the following companies: Argosy, Avco/Solar, Bryna, Cecil B. de Mille, Cinema Artists Inc., Columbia, Essanay, Famous-Players Lasky, William S. Hart, Howard Hughes, Stanley Kramer, Mascot, Malpaso, MGM, Mirisch Monogram, Paramount,

PEA/Gonzales/Constantin, Frank Perry, Rafran/San Marco, Republic, Samuel Bronston, Samuel Goldwyn, Selig, Seven Arts, Stockbridge/Hiller/Cinema Center, Tigon/Curtwell, 20th Century-Fox, UA/Jolly/Constantin/Ocean, United Artists, Universal, Hall Wallis, Walter Wanger, Warner Brothers, C. V. Whitnet Pictures Inc.

Although every effort is being made to trace the present copyright holders, we apologize in advance for any unintentional omission or neglect and will be pleased to insert the appropriate acknowledgment to companies or individuals in any subsequent edition of this publication.

Acknowledgments: Cinema Book Shop, Greg Edwards Archive, Ronald Grant Archive, Joel Finler Collection, Thomas Gicrease Institute, David Hine, Kobal Collection, Library of Congress, National Archives, David Robinson, Al Reuter, Talisman Books, United Artists, Bob Willoughby Collection.